The Thundering Voice of
JOHN L. LEWIS

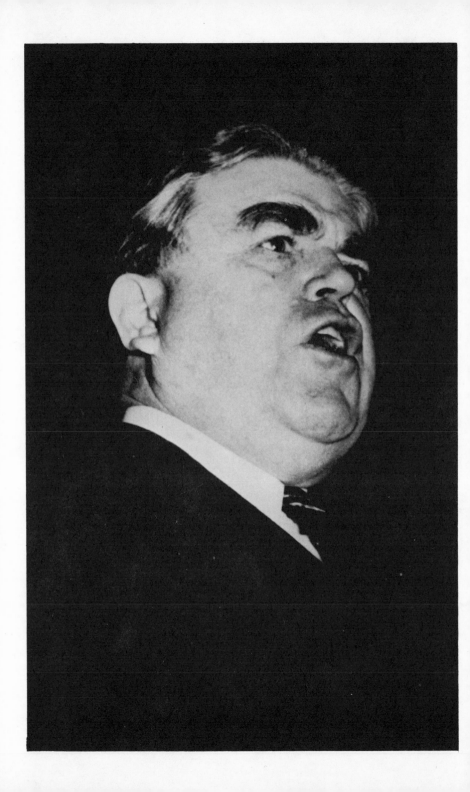

The Thundering Voice
of
JOHN L. LEWIS

by David F. Selvin

Illustrated with photographs

Lothrop, Lee & Shepard Co., New York

Also by DAVID F. SELVIN

Sam Gompers: *Labor's Pioneer*
Eugene Debs: *Rebel, Labor Leader, Prophet*
Sky Full of Storm: *A Brief History of California Labor*
Champions of Labor

To Sue

because once didn't say enough

Contents

1

The Man and His Work

"The name is Lewis"

For more than forty years, he guided the nation's coal miners—in abject defeat and shining victory. He led millions of American workers out of depression and indignity, if not to the promised land, at least to a better land. He was widely hated, frequently denounced, often respected, sometimes commended, and in the end, handsomely praised. Son of a blacklisted miner and a miner himself, he became president of the United Mine Workers at nearly the peak of its strength. The union almost died under the insistent pressures of union-hating employers and a disorganized, impoverished, chaotic coal industry. In this crumbling house, he made himself undisputed master.

While the nation groped its uncertain way from the black depths of the great depression, he built his moldering union into a powerful industrial force. He led millions of American workers in their demands for the simple, democratic opportunity to join unions of their own choice and to bargain collectively with their employers. Under his leadership, great unions captured strategic places in the auto, steel, rubber, and radio industries, and in scores of powerful industries across the land. Their thrust carried the union movement to heights never before achieved.

He clashed with President Wilson and President Harding. Coolidge disappointed him, and Hoover abandoned him. He risked place and power in a bitter feud with Franklin Delano Roosevelt and lost. He quarreled bitterly with Truman. Kennedy admired his "dignity and integrity." Johnson conferred on him the nation's highest civilian honor, the Medal of Freedom.

In the course of World War II, he led his miners into repeated battle against the mine operators and the government. At the time, *Fortune* magazine described him as "the nation's most commonplace 'bad-man' symbol." An overseas Army newspaper cried bitterly, "Speaking for the American soldier, John L. Lewis, damn your coal-black soul." He was endlessly embroiled with the law and the government, attacked by the press, by industry, by other sections of the union movement. Though he seemed always to emerge clutching the prize, his course seemed inevitably to lead to deeper isolation.

He stood over 6 feet tall, weighed about 230 pounds. A newspaperman described his short, powerful arms, "heavy but quick hands, with gnarled, strong fingers. . . . He is remarkably light on his feet, walks with the speed and agility of a cat." His great, swept-back mane of hair, thick jutting eyebrows, and strong-jowled jaw caught the interest of countless photographers and cartoonists. His deep, basso voice was as deliberate and prodding as a ringmaster's whip. His "supple and powerful" mind was "seldom, if ever, clouded by uncertainty or self-doubt," an historian observed. "He who tooteth not his own

John L. Lewis. *National Archives (USIA)*

horn," Lewis sometimes said, "the same shall not be tooted."

Words, to him, were tools. He kept them sharp and shining and used them with surgical skill. He was a master of the insult, the epithet. He once overruled an Irish delegate at a union convention, "I mined coal in Illinois when Delegate Ansbury was herding sheep in Bulgaria." The delegate angrily demanded an apology. Lewis said he was prepared to apologize, not to Delegate Ansbury but to "the committee of twelve Bulgarians" who had protested the suggestion "that such a person as Pat Ansbury could be associated with them." He was unsparing in attack. "They are smiting me hip and thigh," he once cried to reporters. "Right merrily I shall return their blows."

He read widely. His shelves were stacked with volumes on Lincoln (whose birthday he shared), Napoleon and military history, economics, and a supply of detective stories for relaxation. His language was splashed with gleanings from the Bible, Shakespeare, and the poets, and with references to the tactics of Napoleon.

In the hallway of his Virginia home, he kept a miner's pick. He knew the coal-mining industry intimately and in detail. He knew coal prices and freight rates in all their bewildering ramifications. He knew the operators, having dealt with them, large and small, weak and strong, in peace and in war, for more than forty years. Most of all, he knew the miners. Knowing them made him strong.

"I know the psychology of a coal miner," he once told a group of them. "I know about his dreams and his ideals

and trials and tribulations. I have lived with coal miners.
I am one of them. . . .

"I have laid down in a mine tunnel with my face in a
half inch of water, and pulled my shirt up over my head,
expecting to die the next minute in an explosion I heard
coming toward me. And when God performed a miracle
and stopped that explosion before I died, I think it gave
me some understanding of what men think about and
how they suffer when they are waiting to die in a coal-
mine explosion.

"So, I understand some of the thoughts of the coal
miners of America . . . and when I speak, I speak the
thoughts of the membership of the United Mine Workers, because I understand them. I remain true to them
and they remain true to me."

New York Times Reporter A. H. Raskin described, in
The Atlantic, an encounter between Lewis and a West
Virginia mine operator. "I don't understand a man like
you," the operator told Lewis, "with your great talent,
whose sole interest in life is the acquisition of power,
power, and more power."

To Lewis, power was partly a matter of running the
union more efficiently. He knew more about the miners'
problems than anyone else, he once said, worked harder
on them than anyone else; his decisions, therefore, ought
to have meant more than those of anyone else. To an
interviewer who questioned his "pretty heavy power,"
Lewis replied, "Advisory power. Do you know of any
other kind I have besides advisory power?"

"There is no doubt," a *Fortune* writer commented,
"that Lewis is a supreme opportunist who delights in

gathering power unto himself. But it has never been proved that his power has been consciously wielded at the expense of those among the rank and file who trust him." If it hadn't paid off, the writer said, his power would long since have ceased to exist.

Power was only one facet of the man. Historian Arthur Schlesinger, Jr., wrote that his "utterances gave the sorrows and aspirations of all labor a new dignity. Across the country, people recognized in him—some with hope, some with fear—the authentic voice of a great social force."

His powerful voice demanded for the working millions a voice in the decisions that would determine whether there would be food on their dinner tables and would affect the education of their children, the clothing they wore, the pleasure they enjoyed. "Let the workers organize," he proclaimed. "Let the toilers assemble. Let their crystallized voice proclaim their injustices and demand their privileges. Let all thoughtful citizens sustain them, for the future of labor is the future of America."

Lewis told James Wechsler, who wrote a sharply critical biography of him, "Think of me as a coal miner, and you won't make any mistake." He told a union convention, "I come from the coal mines. I have never wandered away from them and the men and women who man the mines in this country. I do not expect to."

He once appeared before a Senate committee. The chairman, realizing that Lewis was known to everyone, asked him to identify himself "for the record."

"The name is Lewis, J. L.," he said, "representing the United Mine Workers of America."

2

The Early Years

"I would count those five years as my education"

"On my father's side," Lewis recalled, "my family were fighters. They roved a great deal. They were very much interested in the world about them. They were tough people. My mother's side of the family was the quiet kind. They were scholars, teachers, sort of retiring and shy."

His father had left his native Wales about 1875. He wandered first to Australia, then to America, settling in the tiny mining town of Lucas, Iowa. There, he went to work digging coal for the White Breast Fuel Company. About that time, the Watkins family left Wales and emigrated, too, to Lucas. In 1878, Tom Lewis and Louisa Watkins were married. To them, on February 12, 1880, a son was born, and they named him John Llewellyn Lewis.

Tom Lewis had been a union man in Wales. The union's collapse had encouraged him to leave. At Lucas, he helped to organize a local assembly of the Knights of Labor, and in 1882, he led them out on strike. Sheer hunger drove them back to the mine, except for Tom Lewis who was blacklisted and was not hired back. He wandered, then, with his growing family, for some fifteen

years. When new management took over the White
Breast mine in 1897, the Lewis family returned to Lucas.

All the time that young John was growing up, he
heard his father's angry denunciation of the operators
and of the miners, too, who had refused to fight when the
owners had blacklisted him. John's formal education,
most of it, he received in Des Moines. He is a "remarkable public speaker," a teacher told his mother, and suggested he study law. As a boy of twelve, he sold newspapers and worked at odd jobs. He left school at fourteen
and went to work digging coal. His job filled eleven hours
a day and more, but he found time for a wide range of
outside activities. He organized and managed a local de-
bating team, played shortstop, and managed a baseball
team. He was offered a chance to get in on the "ground
floor" of the movie business, but he thought 90 dollars
was too much to pay for a share of the local picture
house. He served as secretary of the miners' union in
Charlton, the nearby county seat. Later, he worked as a
partner in a seed business and in a carpentry shop. He
ran the local opera house, where occasional roadshows
and lectures brightened the Lucas scene. He played
poker with a select group of miners and read avidly,
though his reading leaned heavily toward the sensa-
tional. At one point, he considered entering the prize
ring to seek the heavyweight boxing crown.

When Lewis was twenty-one he took a "workingman's
tour" of the Rocky Mountain mining country. He traveled by rail, in passenger cars or on freight cars, according to the contents of his pocketbook. He dug coal in

Colorado, Wyoming, and Montana, copper in Colorado and Arizona, and silver in Utah. When fire struck a Wyoming coal mine, young Lewis helped in the rescue work. A longtime friend remembered, "In 1905 Lewis helped to carry out the cruelly blasted bodies of the two hundred and fifty-six miners in the Union Pacific mine disaster at Hannah, Wyoming.* Lewis was baptized in his own tears when he saw the numb, mute faces of the wives who thus suddenly became widows of the men they loved."

He received a major part of his education, Lewis has recalled, in those five years when he knocked about the country. He saw suffering; he saw people pushed around; he came to know misery among large parts of the population. Those five years did more to shape his feelings and understanding of how people behave, he always said, than anything else in his experience. "Those five years were probably one of the most important parts of my life. . . . I would count those five years as my education."

He returned to Lucas, and in 1907 he married Edith Myrta Bell, daughter of the local doctor and a schoolteacher. She was "a small woman," a reporter later noted, "unobtrusive, sedate and with a great capacity for silence." She was a major force in her husband's life. She suggested books to read, guided him in his studies, helped to polish his public speaking. He discussed his problems with her, counseled with her on his plans. She gave him two daughters, one of whom died when she

* *The U. S. Bureau of Mines records the explosion and fire as taking place June 30, 1903, with a death toll of 169.*

was very young, a son, and a love that brought out, a biographer said, "an unsuspected tenderness in this man seemingly all steel."

In 1909, the young couple moved to Panama, a tiny coal camp deep in southern Illinois. They were followed by Lewis's brothers. Around Lucas, it was said, "Those Lewises—if you lick one of 'em you have to lick them all." With his brothers' help, Lewis was soon elected president of the local miners' union. The state convention in 1910 made him the miners' legislative agent, and he moved to Springfield, the state capital. "Oh, that's just John Lewis," a New York editor remembered being told, "he's always bothering his head about statistics and the miners' union."

His activities caught the attention of Sam Gompers, president of the American Federation of Labor (AFL). Gompers hired him as an AFL field representative. In that capacity, Lewis helped to organize unions in countless plants. He took part in an unsuccessful effort to unionize the employees of the United States Steel Corporation. He was put in charge of the AFL forces in a great copper strike in upper Michigan. He got to know the rubber workers in Akron. He was introduced to the brutal coal and iron police in Pennsylvania. He spoke for the AFL before committees of Congress and many state legislatures.

"He learned the hard way," C. L. Sulzberger wrote of those days, "burning his fingers and callousing his knuckles. He saw starvation. He saw despair." Lewis learned from Gompers how to be a business unionist.

Like Gompers, he rejected the radical philosophies that were popular in some sections of the labor movement. Like Gompers, too, Lewis built his philosophy around practical goals—higher living standards, better conditions, safer cleaner workplaces—not on some far-off tomorrow, but now. These lessons remained the core of Lewis's unionism.

Lewis first attended a miners' convention in 1906 and soon became a familiar figure at these gatherings. On February 1, 1917, President John P. White appointed him statistician of the United Mine Workers. The *United Mine Workers Journal* reported, "He is a man of strong personality, a gifted orator, and his many friends will rejoice to know that he has been appointed statistician of our international organization."

3 /

The Plight of the Miner

"... men who go down into the dangers
of the mines and work together"

English-speaking man has been digging coal for some
seven-hundred years, John L. Lewis once lectured a
miners' convention. "Always," he noted, "the conditions
of the mine workers were bad." Wages, if any at all, were
low. Hours were cruelly long. The air was often foul and
the work dangerous. Employers found it easier and
cheaper, he said, to replace the injured and the dead than
to maintain safe working conditions. At one time, he
added, women worked in the mines. Naked to the waist,
they hauled little cars along dank tunnels or carried
baskets of coal up ladders in the shafts.

Louis Joliet and Father Jacques Marquette reported
the presence of "cole mines" in the United States as
early as 1673. In 1750, coal was being used for heating
and cooking. Soon blacksmiths were using it to cast can-
nonballs for the colonists' artillery. Its real importance,
however, came from the nation's growing industries and
expanding network of rail and water transportation. The
country's mines produced only 108,000 tons of bituminous coal in 1800, and a bare 1,000 tons of anthracite.*

---

*Anthracite coal is nearly pure carbon—hard, black, shining,
slow burning, nearly odorless, high in heat. Bituminous is softer,*

Going into a mine "is not like riding in a subway in New York or elsewhere." *Bureau of Mines, U.S. Department of the Interior*

By 1850, the nation burned some 4 million tons each of hard coal and soft. By 1900, the nation was using 212 million tons of bituminous, 57 million tons of anthracite. In 1850, practically all of the energy that powered the nation's mills and factories came from wood. By 1900, industry was using five times as much energy; coal supplied two-thirds of it. About half a million men and boys dug the nation's coal in about five-thousand mines.

Coal was mined then pretty much as it had been for generations—by a centuries-old hand process. Machinery

contains more moisture and volatile matter. Anthracite is found mainly in Pennsylvania; bituminous underlies more than a score of states, stretching roughly across the nation's beltline.

had only begun to be used. The man-trip carried the miner down the shaft or into the tunnel. It was "no pleasant pastime," Lewis told a wartime labor board. "It is not like riding in a subway in New York or elsewhere."

The cage or open car carried miners "past walls dripping with black water," McAlister Coleman wrote, "into a darkness" that you could "reach out and touch . . . as one fingers black velvet." Naked bulbs specked the darkness of the main haul—the "Main Street" of the mine. Bays along the main haul provided rooms for repair and maintenance shops; once mine mules had been stabled there. Side streets branched out from the main haul and rooms opened off them. The height of each room was usually the thickness of the coal seam, ranging from two to forty feet. Many miners worked their seams on their knees. The roof of a room was supported by pillars or walls of coal and by timbers. At one end glistened the face of coal.

With his "buddy," usually a younger miner learning the trade, the miner was responsible for his room. He set his own pace, worked in his own way, with little or no direction from the boss." The thing about mining," one man said, "is that I can work just as I feel like it." The miner undercut the coal three to six feet deep along the face. He drilled holes into the face, loaded and tamped them with explosives, then blasted the coal. When the smoke cleared, he shoveled the broken-down coal into cars, clearing it of slate and rock as he loaded. Cars were pushed on tracks to a pickup point where they were hauled to the surface. The miner and his buddy were responsible for laying more track as their room expanded, for supporting the roof with timber, often for clearing up rock from cave-ins, and for bailing or pumping water. Sometimes they were paid for the "dead work." Sometimes the company hired day men to do it. The miner's pay was almost always based on the coal he dug and sent to the pithead.

Mines, of course, were opened where the coal was, and the miners clustered around the mines. Typically, the mines are located, Lewis once said, "in a canyon between the mountains and the valley, some two hundred yards in width. The houses are built on the side of the hill;

A miner working his seam. *Bureau of Mines, U.S. Department of the Interior*

there are no public roads because the towns are not incorporated; the coal company owns all the land for miles around. . . . The only buildings are owned by the coal company—the houses, the company store, the post office, and the schools. There is no place of public assemblage." In a coal town, the merchant was usually a coal-company employee, the policeman a company guard. The teacher in the one-room school was hired by the company, the postmaster was a company clerk. There was usually little in the way of recreation facilities; what there was usually was furnished by the company.

For generations, coal diggers were cut off from much of American life, until, in time, movies, radio, and television brought them into closer touch. Isolated in company-dominated towns, battling endlessly against the hazards of his work in underground, sunless "tombs," the miner often saw the outside world as strange and hostile. His separate world created a stubborn independence and a strong sense of solidarity.

Lewis used to say, "The public does not understand and I think never will, that almost spiritual fealty that exists between men who go down into the dangers of the mines and work together—that fealty of understanding and brotherhood that exists in our calling to a more profound degree than in any other industry. The public does not know that a man who works in a coal mine is not afraid of anything except his God; that he is not afraid of injunctions, or politicians, or threats, or denunciations, or verbal castigations, or slander—that he does not fear death."

4

Early Union Activity

"The coal you dig is not Slavish coal, or Polish
coal, or Irish coal. It is coal."

My daddy was a miner
And I'm a miner's son,
And I'll stick with the union
Till ev'ry battle's won.

These words, or something like them, have echoed in
the coal camps for generations. Sung in scores of tongues
to a hillbilly tune or a half-remembered folk song, in
anger and in pride, they signaled the unique solidarity of
the miners.

John Bates organized the first union of miners in this
country in Schuylkill County, Pennsylvania, in 1849. It
soon fell apart in an unsuccessful strike. In 1860, Daniel
Weaver sent out a call: "Men can do jointly what they
cannot do singly; and the union of minds and hands, the
concentration of their power, becomes almost omni-
potent. How long, then, will miners remain isolated?"

The miners formed the American Miners' Association,
but though it survived the Civil War, it collapsed in the
restless and depressed years that followed. Its successor,
John Siney's Workingmen's Benevolent Association, also

faded away. In 1873, though, Siney again sounded the call, "Come and reason together." That winter he was made president of the newly formed Miners National Association of the United States. The union was rocked by the sharp depression of 1873. Strikes broke out, and the union's meager funds were used to buy cornmeal and flour for the strikers. Siney was charged with the crime of assisting in a combination of miners to raise their wages, but he was eventually freed. Union miners were evicted from company houses and fired from their jobs. Some blamed Siney for their trouble and it sat heavily on him. He died soon afterward, a "broken, forsaken man."

In those turbulent years, two secret organizations flourished among the miners. Young, angry Irish immigrants banded together in the Molly Maguires, often accused of repeated acts of violence against their employers. Franklin B. Gowen, a leading anthracite operator, hired the Pinkerton detective agency to infiltrate the Mollies. James McPartland, a Pinkerton agent, made his way into the inner circle and was soon proposing deeds of violence outdoing any the angry miners had thought of. After he was discovered, he became the chief witness against the Mollies. Fourteen miners were hanged.

The Noble Order of the Knights of Labor conducted its affairs behind elaborate religious trappings and in deepest secrecy. It hid its very name from outsiders, using the symbol, ✹✹✹✹✹, or the names, Five Stars or Five Asterisks. Its secrecy was intended to protect the members against their employers' wrath and against "desperate men gaining admission for treachery." In theory, it opposed strikes, but in practice, fought hundreds of them. Dramatic victories in strikes on the railroads of the powerful Jay Gould brought a turbulent flood of new members. No sooner had it reached a peak, though, than its decline began. In less than a dozen years, its influence waned; in another dozen, it was almost forgotten. The Knights wavered between weakness and strength, between boldness and timidity. The Knights, wrote labor historian Norman J. Ware, "were in sympathy with everything and involved in nothing."

Its demise was hurried, too, by its conflict with the rising unions of skilled craftsmen. The unions and the Knights had collaborated to form the Federation of Organized Trades and Labor Unions in 1881 as a national union center. Soon, though, they were in sharp conflict. The divided and failing federation was replaced in 1886 by the American Federation of Labor (AFL) under the tough, pragmatic, energetic Sam Gompers. The Knights attempted to meet the AFL challenge by forming competing unions of its own. One such was a union of coal miners labeled National Trade Assembly 135.

At almost the same time, John McBride, Daniel McLaughlin, and Chris Evans were putting together the National Federation—later the National Progressive Union—of Miners and Mine Laborers. The rival unions wavered between uncertain cooperation and heated competition. Finally, in 1890, they agreed to unite. They formed the United Mine Workers of America (UMW), claiming to speak for some 10,000 miners. They picked

A "room" in a mine. *Bureau of Mines, U.S. Department of the Interior*

John B. Rae, a veteran miner and leader of Assembly 135, as their first president.

Through the UMW, the miners hoped to gain higher living standards and better working conditions. They asked for an eight-hour day. They wanted to be paid for all the coal they produced. When coal was screened at the tipple (where it was unloaded at the head of the mine shaft, or tunnel), the fine stuff went through the screen; the miner was paid for what was left. "We got paid for the chunks," a miner said, "but lost the slack."

They wanted pay for "run of the mine"—all the coal they dug and loaded and sent to the surface. And payment in cash, not scrip, the paper money issued by the company and usually accepted only at the company store, where prices were artificially high. If independent stores accepted scrip, they often took heavy discounts.

The miners called for greater safety precautions, for adequate timbering, ventilation, and drainage. The union pledged itself "to use all honorable means to maintain peace between ourselves and employers; adjusting all differences as far as possible, by arbitration and conciliation, that strikes may become unnecessary."

After a string of unsuccessful strikes, Rae was succeeded as president of the UMW by John McBride in 1892. McBride left to take over the presidency of the AFL in 1894, the one year that Sam Gompers was not re-elected to that office between 1886 and his death in 1924. Phil Penna took McBride's place; Michael Ratchford succeeded him. Under Ratchford, a new interstate agreement established an eight-hour work day starting April 1, 1898. Ever since, April 1 has been a miners' holiday.

Ratchford was appointed to the United States Industrial Commission, and the presidency was taken over by twenty-eight-year-old John Mitchell. Orphaned at six, working on a farm at ten, Mitchell entered the mines when he was twelve. At fifteen he was a member of the Knights of Labor. An early member of the UMW, he climbed the ladder of union offices from subdistrict treasurer to legislative representative, then organizer and vice president. As president, he set himself the task of organizing all the anthracite miners of Pennsylvania.

He found the miners overworked and underpaid, cheated at the tipple and at the company store. He found countless miners who had worked for years without drawing more than a few pennies in cash, living in unending debt to the company store. He found thousands of immigrants—newcomers from Hungary, Poland, Italy, and earlier arrivals from Ireland, Wales, and Scotland —divided by language and custom and nationality and religion. Mitchell preached unity, "The coal you dig is not Slavish coal, or Polish coal, or Irish coal. It is coal." He worked, too, to enlist public opinion, appealing to priests and preachers, editors and educators. Slowly, painfully, he built up a dues-paying membership of some 9,000 anthracite miners.

In 1900, he called them out on strike. Astonishingly, more than 112,000 miners responded. The operators refused to negotiate with the union, but after a few weeks, they posted notices of a 10 percent raise in pay; they abolished the sliding scale that tied wage rates to the price of coal; they recognized the mine committees. So sweeping were the gains that October 29, the day the strike ended, became another miners' holiday, "John Mitchell Day." Mitchell, barely thirty, entered the gallery of miners' heroes.

Again, in 1902, operators refused to negotiate and again, miners—140,000 of them—quit work. Mitchell had offered to cut union demands in half to avert the suffering that a strike would bring. Once more, he appealed to public opinion, to religious leaders, journalists, educators,

and prominent citizens in every walk of life. He proposed
to let three eminent religious leaders decide the dispute.
George F. Baer, spokesman for the operators, replied
icily that "anthracite mining was a business and not a
religious, sentimental, or academic proposition." The
operators, he said, had nothing to arbitrate.

After five months, President Theodore Roosevelt summoned Mitchell and the mine operators to Washington
and urged them to accept arbitration. Baer refused. He
scoffed, too, at the suggestion of suffering among the
miners. "They don't suffer," he said. "Why, they don't
even speak English." Nevertheless, the operators agreed
to arbitrate the dispute if no labor representative sat on
the arbitration board. Roosevelt pondered over the condition, then named the head of the Brotherhood of Railway Conductors to the panel as "an eminent sociologist."

The commission awarded the miners a 10 percent
raise in wages, but reinstated the hated sliding scale. It
gave the miners the right to elect their own checkweigh-
man to end cheating at the tipple. It set up a board to
adjust complaints, and gave the union a place on the
board, though it denied it formal recognition.

Mitchell was widely acclaimed for his astute leadership of the miners. He served as president until 1908,
when he went to work for the National Civic Federation.
This ponderous body united a smattering of industrial
leaders and union officials in an effort to develop conciliation and negotiation in industrial relations. Not all unionists, by any means, saw it as a beneficial undertaking.
Socialists and other radicals often denounced it as a de-

vice to weaken the forces of labor. When Mitchell went
to work for the Federation in 1908, the miners heaped
gifts on him. "God bless you, John," they said. Three
years later, the miners' convention gave him a choice
between retaining his union membership or his job with
the Civic Federation. He gave up the job.

Mitchell was succeeded by Thomas L. Lewis (no rela-
tion to John L. Lewis). His successor, John P. White,
gave John L. his first major union recognition. Lewis
served as acting chairman at the 1916 convention and on
the interstate wage-scale committee. In 1917, White appointed him statistician, then added the duties of business manager of the *Journal*. Lewis also won a place on
the miners' delegation to the conventions of the American Federation of Labor.

In April, 1917, the United States entered World War I.

5

The First Battle

"I will not fight my government"

President Wilson established the Federal Fuel Administration to speed the wartime supply of coal. When the UMW president took a position with the Fuel Administration, Vice President Frank J. Hayes stepped up to the presidency, and Lewis moved up to the vice presidency. Hayes, they said, had little heart for the routine work of the office. Much of it—along with the power of the presidency—was taken over by Lewis.

A wage conference at about that time set a base wage of 5 dollars a day for the miners.

Like all workers, miners were pinched by the wartime rise in prices. The wage rates negotiated in 1917 bought less and less. The Fuel Administration approved a catch-up raise for anthracite miners but turned down another increase for the soft-coal miners. As soon as the fighting stopped in Europe, the soft-coal miners raised the question again.

Although the fighting had stopped, a peace treaty had not been signed and the nation remained technically in a state of war. Wartime food and fuel regulations remained on the books, but the troops were demobilized. The Fuel

Two miners pickaxing in a coal mine, 1917-18. *National Archives (U.S. War Department General Staff photo)*

Administration, like other wartime agencies, was dismantled. Across the nation, people were caught up in an often frantic scramble to get back to the ways of peace. Many, captivated by wartime slogans, called for social and economic revolution; many more feared that it was close at hand. Federal officials raided the halls of radical groups and hundreds were arrested. Strikes broke out in countless industries, most notably the steel industry. The wave of unrest broke and receded after the steelworkers' strike had been smashed, and the nation entered a short but sharp depression.

With Lewis, now acting president, in the chair, a special convention of miners in March, 1919, called for an 8-dollar a day wage, a 6-hour day and 5-day week. In the restless spirit of the time, they called on the Government to take over ownership and operation of the mines. In September, the miners voted that if there were no agreement by November 1, there would be no work. As far as they were concerned, the war was over.

Negotiations made no headway. A statement issued in the name of President Wilson—he was incapacitated by a nervous breakdown and knew nothing of it—called a strike "not only unjustifiable but unlawful." On November 1, nevertheless, the miners stayed home.

War-torn lands in Europe urgently needed coal. The shortage at home mounted rapidly. The Wilson Administration asked a Federal court to order the union to cancel the strike. Judge A. B. Anderson gave the union officers just three days—until six o'clock on November 11, the first anniversary of the Armistice—to call off the walkout.

For some forty-eight hours the miners' General Policy Committee debated the union's response. Alexander Howat, a rebellious union leader from Kansas, damned the judge. "We're not going to be robbed by any legal fiction about the war still going on," he declared, "when even the biggest damn fool in the world can see it's over."

The union's attorney, Henry Warrum, said he could see no way out except to comply. Finally, Lewis settled it, ". . . with as much resentment and bitterness as was in the heart of anybody present," he would "do his duty . . . and cancel the strike order."

He issued the cancellation. The miners stayed home.

On December 3, Judge Anderson charged Lewis and several scores of union representatives with contempt of court. At virtually that moment, Presidential Secretary Joseph Tumulty proposed an immediate, but temporary, increase of 14 percent and appointment of a presidential commission to write the final terms. On December 7, Lewis called off the strike. "I will not fight the government," he told reporters, "the greatest government on earth."

Lewis explained at greater length to a special convention early in 1920. The President's statement calling the strike unjustifiable and unlawful, he said, "changed the scene of battle and our armies were confronted with an opposition of which we had never dreamed. We cared not for the minions and the legions and the cohorts of the coal operators of America; we felt our cause was just . . . but when the government of the United States said that in the interest of the public welfare and the peace and the tranquility of our nation the strike could not be, it behooved honest men to stop, think and wonder whither we were drifting."

In March, 1920, the United States Coal Commission raised the miners' pay, but the daymen were not satisfied. They promptly walked out on strike. Finally, the day rate was boosted to $7.50, to remain in force until April 1, 1922.

Frank Hayes formally retired from the union presidency, and on February 7, 1920, Lewis was made president. Philip Murray was chosen vice president. Murray had been president of the Pittsburgh district and a former member of the UMW International Executive Board, the Union's governing body. Lewis and Murray were opposed in the 1920 union election but won without difficulty.

Lewis, in name now as well as in fact, headed the nation's largest and most powerful union. Its membership numbered close to half a million miners in nearly every coal field in the country. After nearly a year's struggle, it had established a new, higher, wage level, highest in its history. But the coal industry was sick. It very quickly began to show the symptoms of overproduction and falling prices that were to plague it, and the miners, for years to come.

6 |
Defending the Union Wage

"... there must be no backward step"

The operators' response to the 1920 wage scale was direct and violent. In West Virginia, nonunion operators hired armed guards to patrol the coal camps. Union representatives were jailed, beaten, hounded out of town. Shooting erupted; guards, law enforcement officers, miners—some bystanders, too—were killed. Union miners were fired. The deputies forced a growing number of families into the streets, dumping their meager belongings on the side of the road. The evicted miners moved their families into mushrooming tent cities; hunger and suffering became a daily fact. The Red Cross refused to help. No "act of God" was involved, the miners were told. Women set up picket lines when the courts banned the men from picketing. They, too, were jailed, until there was scarcely room for another person in the crude bull pen where they were imprisoned. Still their voices rang out:

> Just like a mule,
> a goddam fool
> will scab until he dies.

The women were finally released when guests in the

hotel across the street complained of the noise. The courts ordered picketing halted, prohibited miners from holding meetings on public roads, and banned their prayer meetings. Mine guards slashed their tents, destroyed food supplies, poured coal oil into their milk.

The Governor declared martial law and armed the mine owners' private detectives as well as the militia. From miles around, angry miners mobilized their supporters. With World War I veterans as the core, they organized a crude military force to march on Logan and Mingo counties. The sheriff recruited a counterforce, and a deadly battle seemed inevitable. An emissary of President Warren Harding unsuccessfully tried to persuade the men to disperse. Firing broke out, but surprisingly, few were hurt. Then the United States Infantry moved in. The union army gave up its weapons, and the men returned to their homes. Union leaders and miners were later indicted, and some were tried on charges of treason and conspiracy growing out of the Mingo county shootings. Most were acquitted, but half a dozen years went by before the last miner was out of jail. The mines in Mingo county remained nonunion.

In the summer of 1921, Lewis ran for the presidency of the American Federation of Labor against Sam Gompers, his one-time boss. Gompers had been defeated only once since 1886, and then by John McBride, president of the UMW. Gompers defeated Lewis with little difficulty. Lewis lost even some of the votes of the delegates from his own union. "I am a good deal like the young man who told his mother he had been called to preach," Lewis commented afterward. "The old mother

Lewis with his wife and daughter Kathryn at the White House. *Library of Congress, Herbert French Collection*

asked him if he was sure it was not some other noise he had heard."

At the turn of the year, the coal industry was in sorry shape, the miners in growing misery. Lewis estimated that a quarter of a million miners, close to half the work force, went without work that winter. In Pennsylvania, miners had been living for more than a year on one to three days of work a week. Conditions reached a miserable low in the final week of the year—the worst "ever known to the coal trade," according to *Black Diamond*, a coal-industry trade journal. Hundreds of mines were shut down; hundreds more were working short hours. Operators were in a position to hire anybody, pay any wage. Wage cuts were frequent throughout the nonunion areas and yet, *Black Diamond* declared, "all of the cutting of wages fails to sell coal."

A Baltimore *Sun* reporter toured the West Virginia towns during the Christmas season. ". . . While nearly all America is thinking of its Christmas dinner," he wrote, "there are children in the little mining town of Minden who have no shoes, and families which have been living on potato-paring soup until their more fortunate neighbors could no longer afford to spare the potato parings." Many families, he found, had no money, no prospects of any. Many had only thin, summer clothing in the freezing mountain air and hardly any coal for their stoves, in a town that lived on coal.

Times could hardly have been more unfavorable for the miners. But in January, 1922, speaking to a convention of anthracite miners, Lewis planted his feet.

"One thing must be sure. . . . In this day there must be no backward step by the mine workers of this country." He explained, "We do not expect to follow the nonunion mine worker down the ladder of wage reductions to the morass of poverty and degradation which prevails below, and we do not propose to have the nonunion yardstick applied to our standards of living." If that means industrial conflict, he said, let it come.

The 1920 contract obligated operators to meet the miners in a joint wage conference. Many operators simply refused. Those who went demanded that the miners take a cut in pay. Not without a fight, the union replied. The union's General Policy Committee set a nationwide coal strike for April 1, 1922. To its strike call, it added, almost as an afterthought, an invitation to miners in the nonunion fields to join the strike.

"Quietly, solidly, without malice, rather carefree," one observer wrote, the miners took their tools from the mines. Games of baseball, handball, and horseshoes broke out in the vacant lots. Idle miners crowded the nearby towns. A good many tended their gardens. Some packed and left to visit their old homes in Europe. But unusual things were happening, too. The *Journal* noted "unusual interest" in union organization among nonunion miners. At one mine, the fireboss—who was not eligible for union membership—handed out the strike call. At another, the superintendent promised to take back a wage cut. "And when will you take back the take back?" the miners asked. At countless mines, the men simply stayed home.

The strikers were often former union members or

sons of union members. Some had belonged to unions in the old country—Wales or Poland or Hungary. To many, the union was the one answer to their troubles. "No money left," a miner said. "Company store got it all." Another added, "These companies never had anything to stop them, so they took all they could."

On March 28, the president of the H. C. Frick Company, satellite of the powerful, nonunion U. S. Steel, had proclaimed, "The miners of the Connellsville coke region will not strike. They are satisfied . . . and will remain loyal." They realized strikes would not bring them anything, he said; "all the paid agitators of the union" would have no effect on them.

By mid-April, though, it was clear that the miners of Connellsville were in full rebellion. Van Bittner, Lewis's special representative in the area, exulted. "The Connellsville coke region is closed down." Forty-thousand men were on strike, the largest nonunion field in the country was organized, he reported.

The revolt reached beyond the coke region. An official circular estimated that nearly 100,000 nonunion men had joined the strike. Lewis hailed their strike as a "splendid achievement." He promised that their hardships and sacrifices "shall not be made in vain." All the power of the union would support them. "Right shall prevail. Humanity must win."

"If we were surprised by the magnitude of our success in pulling out the nonunion men," wrote John Brophy, head of District 2, "the employers were thunderstruck."

The operators put small armies of armed guards into

Lewis as he left the White House, May 4, 1922. *Library of Congress, Herbert French Collection*

the field. With the help of company-dominated town officials, they attempted to block mass meetings or to break them up. One sheriff declared it was his duty "to keep those damned organizers out of the county." Strikers were evicted from company houses, and tent cities sprang up. Chicken coops and other temporary shelters were put to use to provide makeshift roofs over strikers' heads. At one mine, the company cut off the miners' water supply.

"This is a conspiracy," the operators complained to the courts. They argued that persuading their employees to quit was illegal. To support their stand, they cited the Hitchman case. There, the United States Supreme Court had upheld the "yellow-dog" contract, an agreement by the miner that in return for a job, he would not join a union. When the union sought to induce men to join, the court ruled that it encouraged a "breach of contract" and injured the employer. The union argued in vain that it sought only to improve living and working conditions, that these were lawful purposes, and their strike, therefore, was a lawful strike. The operators got their injunctions, sweeping orders that left strikers helpless.

To the west, in Williamson county, Illinois, the strikers had not bothered to picket the mines. Not for years had the operators attempted to bring in strikebreakers. One operator, though, William J. Lester, had worked out an arrangement with the union for stockpiling coal; he agreed none would be shipped until the strike was settled. His superintendent, C. K. McDowell, however, had other ideas. He relied on members of a small, independent union to operate the giant shovel that stripped away the dirt over the coal seam. He brought in a number of strikebreakers and armed guards. Then McDowell started loading cars for shipping.

He paid no heed to the sheriff's warnings. To union protests, McDowell said he was working the mine with union men, members of the Steam Shovel Men's Union. The subdistrict asked Lewis about the union. Lewis replied that it had been suspended from the American Federation of Labor, that it was furnishing steam-shovel operators in Ohio to work with strikebreakers under armed guards. "Representatives of our organization are justified in treating this crowd as an outlaw organization and in viewing its members in the same light as they do any other common strikebreakers."

On June 21, 1922, McAlister Coleman wrote, a miner had been shot by a high-powered rifle from the bank around the mine. The *Journal* said a number of men, "reported to be striking miners," had gone to the mine to ask the strikebreakers to quit work. The company guards opened fire and killed two of the men. Other striking miners read Lewis's telegram as an invitation to attack these "outlaws" and "common strikebreakers."

By sundown that night, an army of a thousand or more men gathered in the cornfields surrounding the mine. A plane dropped dynamite on the besieged mine. As the men advanced across the fields, armed with bird guns and deer rifles, a machine gun opened fire and continued spasmodically through the night. The pumping station was blown up; a car of food for the strikebreakers was dynamited. When the sun rose, a white flag flew from the mine. The miners and their sympathizers climbed the bank with a whoop and a holler. The giant shovel was blown up, along with several cars loaded with coal. The guards and strikebreakers were lined up to be marched to the nearby town of Herrin.

Someone asked who had fired the machine gun. When the man was pointed out, he was promply killed, his body draped over the silent weapon. McDowell was taken from line and shot. Then the mob took over. Men were chased, assaulted, then shot. Others were stoned, clubbed, beaten, forced to run brutal gauntlets of angry people. The total dead was put close to forty.

The utter brutality of the massacre stunned the nation. Cries for retribution against the union were loud and angry. Lewis indignantly denied having any part in the affair. The union "never encouraged and does not condone lawlessness of any character." He suggested "sinister influences" had been at work, secret operatives, perhaps, hired to provoke violence. As for his telegram, it was intended simply to place these men in the "category of strikebreakers."

By mid-July the nation's coal stocks were depleted. President Harding proposed arbitration, but not for the nonunion areas. The operators rejected the President's suggestion that a study commission be established to set wages and methods of keeping peace in the industry. President Harding then invited the operators to return to their homes and resume operations. The union saw it as an open invitation, backed by militia or Federal troops, to smash their strike.

Lewis invited operators in the old Interstate Joint Wage Conference to meet him in Cleveland. Only a few operators, and then only the smaller ones, accepted. Nevertheless, with this handful, Lewis reached an agreement to end the strike. The miners would go back to work at the old wage scale.

John Brophy and a few of his associates on the General Policy Committee opposed the settlement. They argued vehemently that the union should settle with no operator until it could settle with all. At least, the union should sign no agreement that did not cover all of an operator's mines, both union and nonunion. But they stood alone. Lewis argued that miners on the job could offer even greater support to those remaining on strike. Operators of union mines, too, could invade the markets of the struck mines. Lewis had his way; most of the operators signed for only those mines that had been unionized before the strike.

To the nonunion men who remained on strike, Lewis pledged "the full moral and financial influence" of the union. In Fayette county, operators were reported to be posting thirty-three to thirty-eight percent pay increases —"bitter gasps," the *Journal* called them, to fool the striking miners into returning to work. Still, 25,000 newly organized men stayed out. Many were living in tents. State police, mine guards, deputies, and gunmen patrolled the strike areas. The union was plastered with injunctions.

A less solemn Lewis with an unidentified man at the White House. *Library of Congress, Herbert French Collection*

Miners from Windber, Pennsylvania, "bug lamps" flickering on their old mine caps, set up their picket line in Wall Street in New York City. Their wives told of the high prices they paid at the company stores, how miners were living in tents and chicken coops. Mayor John F. Hylan sent a committee to Windber, where mines produced coal for New York's Interborough Rapid Transit, to verify the miners' charges. The committee reported that the miners had not exaggerated. The miners were kept, it said, "in bondage worse than serfs in Russia or the slaves before the Civil War."

In January, 1923, the Executive Board ended its support of the strike. In August, after seventeen months, District 2 ended the strike in Somerset County, not because of any defects in unionism, the Executive Board said, but because of "the brutal tactics and the tremendous financial strength of the coal companies."

In all, the strikes of 1922 and 1923 cost the union some 4 million dollars. To the 1924 convention, Vice President Murray acknowledged the contribution of the nonunion miners to "the success of our recent strike." It did not bring them "a complete realization of the many things they were trying to secure" but, he maintained, it did improve their wages, despite the lack of a union contract. Brophy and numerous others, then and since, accused Lewis of abandoning the nonunion miners who had responded to the union's call. "A colossal blunder," Brophy wrote.

Lewis told a district convention, "There is only one labor organization in the United States not compelled to take a reduction in wages. That is the United Mine

Workers." He boasted that it was "the single greatest victory ever won by a union engaged in strike or lockout up to that period."

If it was, in fact, a victory, it was a costly one. It sapped the union's strength in men and money and, most of all, in mines. It was driven out of large sections of the nation's coal fields, a prelude to the loss of even more ground in the years ahead. The competition of the nonunion mines would give the miners their darkest hours.

September 15, 1922. *United Mine Workers of America*

He Brings Home the Bacon

7 |
The Losing Fight

"... nothing to discuss with the miners. ..."

"The best wage and working agreement that ever was negotiated," according to the *Journal*, was signed on February 19, 1924, at Jacksonville, Florida. The agreement was sealed at a dinner party, hosted by a Midwestern utilities magnate, with Secretary of Commerce Hoover, a banker, a judge, and the head of the Associated Press among the guests. It extended the wages and conditions of the old contract, based on a $7.50 a day wage, for three more years. "A red-letter day," the *Journal* cried.

Both sides had gone to Jacksonville with strong misgivings. The coal industry could produce "twice as much coal as the country could burn," a union-sponsored history said, "and there were twice as many miners as were needed waiting around for a chance to dig it." The output of nonunion mines, dug at substantially lower wages, was rising steadily. The operators attended reluctantly—some only because Secretary of Commerce Herbert Hoover encouraged them to do so. Once there, they insisted that wages must be cut.

The bituminous industry had just been through a big

Lewis with Gompers (far right) and others. *Library of Congress, Herbert French Collection*

year; industrial production appeared to be climbing; business was good and getting better. Lewis argued that high wages would drive out of the industry those mines that stayed in business only because their operators paid low wages.

That winter, Sam Gompers died. Three years before that Lewis had run for the presidency of the AFL; now,

A Good Day's Work

March 1, 1924. *United Mine Workers of America*

as head of its largest affiliate, he might have pressed a claim to the post. But he faced the vigorous opposition of Matthew Woll, dapper head of the Photo Engravers' Union, commonly considered Gomper's "crown prince," and of James Duncan, aging first vice president. Instead, he threw his decisive support to William Green, secretary-treasurer of the United Mine Workers, who became the new president of the AFL.

As a young man William Green left the mines in Ohio to work in the union. He served in the Ohio State Senate as well. In 1911, he became UMW statistician and two years later took over the secretary-treasurer's post. Green had sometimes differed with Lewis, but in the main he had been a faithful supporter. He had nominated Lewis for his ill-fated run for the AFL presidency in 1921. For years, Lewis returned the favor by nominating Green for the position.

After nearly a year's trial under the Jacksonville rates, operators complained that they could not compete against nonunion coal. Lewis insisted they were legally and morally bound by the Jacksonville agreement. Moreover, wage cuts would not solve the industry's problems.

In June, 1925, however, Consolidation Coal Company, a major producer in the Pittsburgh area, notified the union that it would no longer be bound by the Jacksonville contract. Pittsburgh Coal Company, largest of the commercial producers, shut down its mines, then invited the men to return to work at wage rates based on 6 dollars a day. The agreement was being treated like a "scrap of paper," Lewis complained. He pointed a chunky finger at the aristocratic figure of Andrew Mellon, ". . . perhaps," he said, "the greatest Secretary of the Treasury since the days of Alexander Hamilton. Yet he permits his coal company . . . to violate a contract with the United Mine Workers of America without, in so far as I know, any protest on his part. What a remarkable difference between the private and business morals of a great captain of industry."

Later, A. J. Morrow, president of Pittsburgh Coal,

explained to a Senate committee that the agreement had not been legally or morally binding, but was merely "an arrangement" the company could ignore if it saw fit. Another Pittsburgh official admitted that perhaps the company had been bound "ethically" by its contract. "But economically," he added, "we couldn't live up to it. It meant bankruptcy on account of the competition with the nonunion mines of West Virginia. We had to terminate it."

Lewis complained to President Calvin Coolidge. The Federal Government had used its "influence" to bring about the Jacksonville settlement. Now, he asked the President, would the Government intervene "to maintain the morality and integrity of the existing agreement?" Coolidge replied that he deplored the breaking of any contract, but the arm of government concerned with enforcement of contracts was the courts. He suggested the union seek an "authoritative" ruling.

On September 1, 1925, the anthracite miners quit work. The strike dragged on stubbornly for 165 days. Finally, Governor Pinchot of Pennsylvania got the parties to agree on a new five-year contract. It kept the old wage scale but allowed either party to reopen the question of wages once a year. Little as it seemed at the time, it was this contract that ultimately did so much to save the union.

Meantime, cancellation of the soft-coal contract spread like a contagious disease. Miners struck repeatedly. The companies hired strikebreakers and fenced them in with barbed-wire, searchlights, and ma-

chine-gun towers. When Lewis toured the northern West
Virginia coal towns, he was blanketed with court injunctions. Miners had a right, the courts maintained, to
work on any terms that seemed proper to them—no matter what the terms were. This theory, based on the
Hitchman and Red Jacket cases, produced a bumper
crop of antiunion injunctions and effectively insulated
thousands of miners from any contact with the union.

Lewis told the miners' convention in 1930 that in the
preceding ten years, the union's legal department had
defended some 650 injunction-suits and 6,000 eviction
suits. It had been sued for more than 40 million dollars
in damages. It had spent more than 8 million dollars on
its legal battles. In 1926, the miners had tried to find
out, as the *Journal* put it, whether the law worked both
ways. The union asked a West Virginia court to prohibit
a coal company from repudiating its contract and from
evicting employees and their families from company
houses. The court refused to interfere.

Wages in West Virginia mines, a UMW representative
reported, fell below pre-World War I levels. Nor had
sharp pay cuts increased the amount of time the men
worked. "Gradually," he reported, "general depression
is settling over the district."

Nonunion conditions took over more and more of
the nation's soft-coal mines. John Brophy, now in full
cry against the Lewis administration, contended that
two thirds of the country's soft coal came from nonunion
miners. Lewis admitted that at least 40 percent was
nonunion. The going rate in nonunion mines was close to

3 dollars a day. Most of the nation's coal was dug by men working only two or three days a week. To make matters worse, modern methods and competitive fuels—oil, gas, hydroelectric power—were biting into coal's share of energy production. "Next to a scab," said a union organizer, "in my opinion, the lowest form of human life is an oilburner salesman or a big dam builder."

When the 1927 wage conference took place, a good many operators who had been at Jacksonville in 1924 stayed away. Those who showed up insisted on wage rates that were "continuously competitive" with wages in the nonunion southern mines. The miners vowed that they would not let their wages be set "by the meanest, most unfair, nonunion employer." They were ready to cooperate in seeking answers to the industry's problems, but they insisted a pay cut would solve none of them. The conference broke up. The union was no more successful in signing up individual districts or operators. On April 1, 1927, 175,000 miners quit work. This time, though, the nonunion mines continued to dig coal.

After six months, the miners in Illinois and a few other fields went back to work. In Pennsylvania, parts of West Virginia and Ohio, the strike went on: "A gigantic army of seven hundred and fifty thousand souls," Lewis said, "who have no hope of life and no protection for the future except that which might be accorded them by the United Mine Workers of America."

Lowell M. Limpus, a reporter for the New York *Daily News*, toured the "strike-cursed towns" of Pennsylvania. "We saw thousands of women and children literally starving to death," he wrote. "We found hundreds of destitute families living in crudely constructed bare board shacks. . . . We unearthed a system of despotic tyranny . . . police brutality . . . industrial slavery. . . .

"We located machine guns and tear-gas bombs, prepared to back up the ready rifles that wait to crush any

February 1, 1927. *United Mine Workers of America*

The Convention Is Now in Session

rebellion of hunger-crazed men. And nearby we heard the children of these men—striking miners—crying for food in empty kitchens."

An injunction in West Virginia forbade strikers to advertise their strike by word or poster. A Pennsylvania judge prohibited meeting and singing at any place within hearing of scabs entering or leaving the mine. One judge required pickets to be English-speaking American citizens. Miners' wives, protesting their husbands' arrests, were themselves arrested. Even the Coal River Collieries, owned by the membership of the Brotherhood of Locomotive Engineers, went nonunion. It imported strikebreakers and evicted union miners from the company-owned houses when they refused to take a pay cut. Not all the persuasion of the union movement could change the Brotherhood's stand.

The miners' anguished complaints prompted an investigation by a Senate subcommittee. The operators made their position clear. "We are working on an open-shop basis," the chairman of Pittsburgh Coal said, "and have nothing to discuss with the miners." He added, "That is our answer today . . . tomorrow, next week, next month, in two months or six months."

Henry Warrum, the United Mine Workers' chief counsel, drafted a bill putting the coal industry under Government regulation. The bill would license coal operators, encourage mergers, and form marketing agencies outside the antitrust laws. It also declared labor's right to organize and bargain collectively, a historic forerunner of famed Section 7a and the Wagner Act. Congress ignored the bill.

In mid-July, 1928, some fifteen and a half months after the strike's start, the union's Policy Committee told the districts to make whatever deal they could with their employers. That was the miners' contribution to stabilization of the industry, the *Journal* editorialized. "Now let the operators and the public do as much." Stabilization quickly took place, on a substantially lower level. Wages were cut one third in Ohio, nearly 20 percent in Illinois and Indiana. The Iowa basic rate dropped to $5.80 a day. Reductions ranged from 17 to 33 percent.

The union's eight-year fight to maintain its $7.50 a day basic wage was lost, its treasury drained, its membership depleted. Nonunion miners were digging an increasing part of the nation's coal; many, probably most, of the bituminous miners had been forced out of the union. The operators' determined drive to break the union's standards, if not to destroy the union itself, had attained a new peak of ferocity. Still, Lewis's and the miners' most desperate hours were ahead of them.

8 /
Lewis's First Decade

"Discontents, malcontents, oppositionists, obstructionists, brawlers. . . ."

John L. Lewis never lacked enemies. When he was not battling the operators or denouncing the railroads or belaboring a handy politician, his opponents in the union provided convenient targets. Differences in policies and personalities provoked strong disputes. None was stronger than that over his powers as president.

The tightening ring of nonunion mines had forced the union into an unending fight to survive. It lived for years in a state of almost perpetual crisis. Frequent and lengthy strikes thrust increasing power into Lewis's hands. Power rose to the top, too, from the very size and geographical distribution of the union. Its conventions brought together some fifteen hundred to two thousand delegates in an often clumsy, tumultuous, hectic, and inefficient legislature. Between conventions, communication was often slow and awkward. The UMW was made up of hundreds of local unions, scattered in the canyons and along the hills where the coal veins run, isolated from each other and from the international union office. Economically, too, broad regional, if not national, contracts seemed more fitting; the excuse for local bargaining grew increasingly feeble.

Lewis welcomed, even encouraged, the accumulation of power. It fed his personal appetite, but he also saw it as the efficient way to run the union. Lewis maintained control through a union-wide political machine. He appointed an increasing number of field representatives and district officials. At times, a majority of the International Executive Board was made up of Lewis appointees. At times, too, as many as two-thirds of the districts were under provisional governments named by Lewis.

He did not gain his power without a fight. Districts and local unions put a high price on their autonomy and vigorously defended it. Ambitious men hungered for greater power; local autonomy offered them an appealing platform. The contest between the president's power and local autonomy was fought and re-fought endlessly, most of the time yielding the same result: Lewis ran the union with an increasingly strong hand.

The fight for power was somewhere in the background in practically every convention Lewis presided over in his first fifteen years as president. They were stormy sessions, the McDonald union history recalled. "May the chair state," Lewis roared after a barrage of boos and hisses on one occasion, "you may shout until you meet each other in hell and he will not change his ruling."

"If there are delegates who feel inclined to insult the chairman," he told another convention, "let them step up here on the platform and try it." His firmness was sometimes touched with humor. "For what purpose does the delegate arise?" he asked an objector.

"I want to go on record——"

"If you want to go on record," Lewis interrupted, "write it down on a slip of paper and hand it to the secretary."

Alex Howat, chief of the union's Kansas district, was a major Lewis opponent. He had been accused of taking bribe money from the operators. He had served time in jail for calling a series of strikes in defiance of an antistrike law. He had voted against Lewis in his attempt to unseat Gompers in 1921. He had run against Philip Murray, an ardent Lewis man, for the union's vice presidency. He had displayed an independent and frequently rebellious resistance to the international union's discipline. Lewis had replaced him and his district officers and subsequently expelled him from the union. Howat fought to stay in. The 1924 convention refused to hear his appeal. He walked—some said he charged—down the aisle.

"Alexander Howat, you are not recognized," Lewis thundered, but Howat persisted. The convention broke into ear-splitting pandemonium as Howat climbed the stage and his supporters surged forward in an angry mass. The sergeant-at-arms threw Howat bodily off the platform into the arms of his onrushing friends.

Like Howat, Frank Farrington, head of the influential Illinois district, had voted against Lewis in the AFL presidential contest. Farrington opposed Lewis's efforts to vest greater authority in the international union. He frequently attempted to separate bargaining in Illinois from that of the other districts. He was a vigorous advocate of local autonomy.

John L. Lewis, January 4, 1926. *Library of Congress, Herbert French Collection*

In 1926, Lewis revealed that Farrington had signed a three-year contract with the Peabody Coal Company, a major Illinois producer, to serve as its labor representative at 25,000 dollars a year. The International Executive Board cabled Farrington, who was in Europe attending an international miners' meeting, to return at once to stand trial or resign. Farrington cabled back that he would not resign, and challenged the right of the Board to demand his resignation. The Board, however, suspended him and installed Vice President Harry Fishwick in his place.

The strongest challenge to Lewis's growing power came in 1926 from John Brophy, the scrappy little president of District 2. His lengthening list of complaints against Lewis finally added up to sharply contrasting goals for the union and the industry. Their differences reached a peak in 1926 when Brophy, heading what came to be called the Save the Union Committee, ran against Lewis for the presidency.

Brophy had supported Lewis in his race against Gompers only because at the time Lewis had seemed to favor nationalization of coal. But in 1925, Lewis published a book totally repudiating the idea, putting the two men in sharp opposition to each other. Brophy claimed that in settling the 1922 strike, Lewis had abandoned nonunion miners, many of whom had been in Brophy's district. He resented what he considered Lewis's political intrusions into District 2. He pointed to great areas—West Virginia, Tennessee, Alabama, Colorado, and more—that had been lost to the union.

Brophy's campaign gave voice to the rising discontent

in the union, echoed the threat of the nonunion fields, and dramatized the miners' dissatisfaction with part-time work and low earnings, with company stores and company houses. Brophy tried to make Lewis the butt of the unrest. Lewis, in turn, charged Brophy with disruption and trafficking with outsiders—from Capitalists to Communists. He told the AFL convention that Brophy's campaign was part of a "Bolshevik plot."

The vote was announced as 173,323 for Lewis, 60,661 for Brophy. Nobody was surprised at the result, Brophy wrote later, "but I was a little surprised that they had admitted to that large a vote for me." Brophy and his followers insisted that the election had been stolen.

Lewis's response to Brophy's challenge—the label of Communist or "Bolshevik," the charge of a "plot"—became standard weapons in his arsenal. In 1923, the *Journal* published a series of special articles claiming to expose "the attempt that is being made by red forces, under the direct supervision of Moscow, to seize control of the organized labor movement of America and to use it as a base from which to carry on the Communist effort for the overthrow of the American government."

Communists succeeded in taking over the union's Nova Scotia district. When they called a sympathetic strike in violation of their contract, Lewis quickly ousted them. Communists rallied behind Brophy's campaign and the Save the Union Committee. In 1928, Brophy and others were expelled. Remnants of the Committee, though not Brophy, formed the National Miners Union and affiliated with the Red International of Trade Unions.

The influence of the left wing, never great, was lessened in the years that followed. The UMW barred Communists from membership in the union; it also barred other radicals, members of the Chamber of Commerce, and, later, members of Fascist organizations. Lewis often boasted of his long-standing opposition to Communists and communism, citing the union's bars against them and the *Journal*'s articles exposing them.

In the fall of 1929, Lewis attempted to replace the officers of District 12 in Illinois. District 12 obtained a court order prohibiting him from interfering in its affairs. The conflict led to a fierce struggle for power and, in turn, to the calling of two conventions of coal miners on the same day in March, 1930.

One met in Springfield, Illinois. The call had been signed by the Fishwick group in District 12, along with John Brophy, Alex Howat, Powers Hapgood, Allan Haywood, Adolph Germer, John H. Walker, all onetime opponents of Lewis, most of them expelled members of the union. Their call charged that Lewis's administration had been "an unbroken series of defeats," plunging hundreds of thousands of miners and their families into "poverty and destitution." It charged that Lewis stole elections, packed conventions, and had delegates slugged. "John L. Lewis killed more than the United Mine Workers of America," it accused. "He killed more than the leaders of our union. He killed its very soul." Their convention claimed to represent the only United Mine Workers of America.

On the same day, at Indianapolis, Lewis convened a special convention of NEED AND NECESSITY. The "scab convention," the *Journal* reported, was "a convention of discontents, malcontents, oppositionists, obstructionists, brawlers, wranglers, branglers, moral contortionists, kickers, janglers, whoopers, soreheads, squallers, bellyachers, bunglers, marplots, doublecrossers, destructionists, union wreckers, disappointed office seekers and traitors." The Indianapolis convention reaffirmed Lewis's actions, readopted the international constitution, and expelled the participants in the Springfield meeting who had not already been ousted. It heard William Green, president of the AFL, declare it the only recognized union of miners.

Slightly less than a year later, a court upheld Lewis's claim that the international constitution had been in full force and that District 12 was bound by it. But the court also reinstated District 12's suspended charter and confirmed recently elected district officials. Peace was formally restored, but a still-dissident group withdrew and formed the Progressive Miners of America. It managed to sign up a few mines and remained a small but irritating thorn in Lewis's paw for several years to come.

The 1930 convention, with most of Lewis's usual opponents absent, gave him even broader powers. It involved no fundamental principle, Lewis insisted. It was a choice between making the union more effective or sacrificing efficiency to gain "a little more academic freedom."

By the end of the decade, Lewis held union power firmly in his hands, his opposition mostly vanquished. But the union he dominated was only a faint shadow of what it had once been.

9 /

Depression in the Mines

"... if a thing is busted it don't get goin' agin'"

If a man worked steadily in the 1920's he could get by. He brought home no luxuries; food, clothing, and housing were of the plainest sort. He seldom was able to put aside much for the proverbial "rainy day." Many millions of American workers lived at such a simple, hand-to-mouth level. A good many more, though, never got full-time work. Seasonal layoffs, temporary gluts of the market, bad weather forced them into frequent periods of temporary idleness.

For the miners, though, idleness became a way of life. Shut-down mines, part-time work, low pay spread poverty and hardship through the coal towns. Three-quarters of a million men had worked in the country's coal mines in 1921. By 1929, something between 177,000 and 221,000 had been squeezed out. Silent tipples stood like "industrial tombstones" over dead mines. Weeds covered railroad sidings; mine buildings crumbled; brush and scrub oak took over the land.

After the Jacksonville scale was abandoned, miners worked for what they could get. Nonunion mines paid $2.50 to $5 a day. Union wages, where they survived, were a third or more below the former $7.50 a day.

The unemployed. *Bureau of Mines, U.S. Department of the Interior*

Depression and unemployment were ugly realities for the miners long before they became familiar words to millions of other Americans. But then, unemployment, depression, grinding poverty, and hopelessness spread into every corner of the country. A million and a half American workers were looking for jobs in 1929. The number nearly tripled in 1930, doubled again in 1931.

By 1932, some 12 million were out of work. Thirteen—some say as many as 15—million were unemployed in 1933. The average full-time factory worker had earned 1,306 dollars in 1921; by 1929, he was making 1,508 dollars. By 1933, though, his earnings had been cut to 1,002 dollars. Millions had only part-time work; many millions more had no work at all.

"I ain't had a regular job for four years," a miner said. "When a man has been out of work as long as I have he loses his heart to try to do anything."

Another said, "My earnings are being held for rent. We've had no food for four days."

One miner told of earning 2 dollars in scrip in a month. "In the eight months I've been here," he said, "I've had only one dollar and twenty-nine cents in cash."

A teacher told of asking a girl if she were sick. "No," the girl replied, "just hungry."

The teacher suggested the girl go home and get something to eat.

"It won't do me any good," the girl said. "This is sister's day to eat."

"I'll steal before I starve," was heard more frequently in the coal towns.

"The good Lord or the government has got to do something," a miner said, "so us poor mining folks can make a living. We've stood just about all we can."

In Kanawha county, West Virginia, the company store charged 40 cents a pound for bacon that cost 20 cents at the local chain store. In Perrin county, Kentucky, lard was 6 to 8 cents a pound at the chain store, 15 cents at the company store. Sugar and salt cost just twice as much at the company store as at the outside store.

"There's more money in mining the miners at the company store," a miner grumbled, "than in digging coal out of the ground." The rule was, miners said, "if you can

A street in a mining town. *Bureau of Mines, U.S. Department of the Interior*

buy cheaper somewhere else, you can go and work there, too."

Miners lived in grimy little shacks, Lewis once wrote, "perched on posts that remind one of long rickety legs of ill-nourished slum children . . . clustered higgledy-piggledy in some gulch, along the bank of a polluted little stream. The shanties lean over as if intoxicated by the smoke and fumes of nearby mills."

"Neither words nor pictures," the United States Coal Commission reported, "can portray the atmosphere of abandoned dejection or reproduce the smells."

Usually, the miner was tied even to these mean little houses by stringent leases. He could have no guest who was "objectionable to the company." He gave the company the right to search the house for "improper or suspicious persons." The miner and his family could use the roads, but could not allow anybody else to use them. One lease spelled it out: only the miner and his family, a drayman moving the family in or out, an undertaker and hearse, and family friends in case of death. If the miner went on strike he could be evicted. Where the company did not evict, it sometimes turned off the water. In one case, it removed the roof. The courts ruled that such stringent leases were binding because, they said, the miners "freely" agreed to their terms.

In July, 1930, the anthracite districts renewed their contract for another five years. Wage rates remained unchanged. Work was slack in the anthracite mines, as it was in other coal mines, but the men who worked there were union members. They, and their union dues, supplied a firm base for the otherwise seriously weakened union. Soon after, the union signed a contract with the Pittsburgh Terminal Coal Corporation, its first since the 1927 strike. From West Virginia, Ohio, and Kentucky came stirrings of organizing.

In Harlan, Kentucky, though, efforts of the miners to organize provoked what Louis Stark, in *The New York Times*, labeled "industrial war."

"Coal property has been destroyed," he wrote. "Tipples have been burned, head mine houses dynamited; a miners' relief soup kitchen, supported by communists, was blown to bits . . . and union sympathizers have been beaten up and driven from the country." The war took a dozen lives: deputies serving as mine guards, miners, two reporters.

Stark reported that the operators vowed to fight off the union "with all the weapons they can muster." It was a powerful arsenal: deputies armed with rifles and machine guns; the political and judicial machinery of the county; sheer physical domination of the miners living in company-owned camps. It made it possible for the operators to offer lower prices on their coal. To the miners it brought an almost total denial of civil and constitutional rights, "a virtual reign of terror."

"Children in these communities beg of strangers," Stark reported. "Fathers, unable to find work, cannot buy school books or clothes for them. Some children have to remain at home and others go to school without food. Principals report many in school without breakfast or lunch."

The UMW officers summed up the near-desperate situation for the convention that met in January, 1932: Seven million workers were unemployed. [In fact, the number was probably over ten million by then.] Wage cuts had drastically reduced annual earnings. Farm income was down 29 percent. Home-building was at a standstill and mortgage foreclosures were the order of the day.

Business failures in 1931 broke all records and 1,556 banks had closed their doors. Wage cutting, the report went on, destroyed the purchasing power of "America's best customer." The masses did not have the earning power to buy back prosperity. Nor could the nation's leaders "offer a practical solution for restoration of normal industrial activity."

By 1928, according to *Coal and Unionism* by McDonald, "the once powerful United Mine Workers of America was only a skeleton in the Appalachian area." John Brophy claimed that, by 1930, "coal mining was practically an open-shop industry." Secretary-Treasurer Thomas Kennedy told the convention that year that the union had 293 dues-paying members in western Pennsylvania, where it once had 45,000. It had 512 of a possible 100,000 in West Virginia. But it had 100,000 dues-paying members in anthracite.

In 1931, though, Lewis insisted that "Our organization has preserved itself. No one saved it. . . . It has lived through its winter of discontent." He conceded—though it sounded more like an accusation—that two thirds of the nation's soft-coal industry had cut wages and estab-

A miner's children. *Bureau of Mines, U.S. Department of the Interior*

lished "semi-serf labor relations," enslaved coal miners and impoverished coal-mining communities. And this, he added, despite union "sacrifices" of some 30 million dollars between 1920 and 1930.

Delegates at the 1932 convention challenged Lewis's "no backward step" policy. It had brought calamity to the industry, they claimed. "I never thought," Lewis replied, "that I would have to stand upon the platform in a convention of the United Mine Workers of America and defend myself for opposing wage reductions. . . . I have no apologies to make. I admit . . . I proclaim the fact that I am against wage reductions, have been, and will be." They would solve none of the nation's economic problems. They would be no help to the working man, "put no bread in a child's mouth, nor do they provide shelter for a working man's family."

Lewis was challenged, too, for failing to organize the soft-coal fields. Lewis reminded his critics that the union had spent over 2½ million dollars in three years in Mingo county, West Virginia, "supporting those men, in housing and feeding them, in clothing them, in furnishing them medicine, attending to the children in the hovel where they were born and burying their dead when they died."

"We have found," he said, "that the coal operators, if they would fight long enough and use up enough money, could eventually starve our people beyond the point of further endurance."

Still, one miner shook his head and said, "A miner is no good without a union. But the union couldn't get any place in this depression." Another said, "I don't think the United Mine Workers will ever get goin' agin' . . . if a thing is busted it don't get goin' agin'." And another, "The United Mine Workers will never be any good till they get a new head."

Looking back a few years later, *Fortune* labeled Lewis "labor's most conspicuous flop." His thirteen-year tenure corresponded with the utter demoralization of the industry, the magazine said, "and his union, which was the largest and proudest in America when he took it over, became demoralized along with it."

Another critic observed: "As [1932] neared its end Lewis was triumphant over his union enemies, but the domain over which he presided was a dreary wasteland. He had won uncontested rule of a ruined union. He had built a machine and lost a movement."

10/
The Depression Deepens

"The people are wondering . . . hoping and praying"

Almost everybody agreed that the coal industry was sick, but few agreed on either the cause or the cure. John L. Lewis offered a short and simple explanation: too many mines, too many miners. Operators blamed high wages and discriminatory freight rates. The union blamed "incompetent, inefficient, backward, lazy, disunited" management. Proposed cures ranged from total government control to no control at all.

During World War I, high prices and coal-hungry industries attracted new investments to the coal industry, and thousands of new mines were opened. When peacetime demand fell, some mines went out of production. Most of them, though, did anything, everything they could, to sell coal. Even if they lost money, they continued to sell coal. Whatever price they got helped to pay interest, depreciation, depletion, costs they would have had to bear even if the mine were closed down. It also kept the mines from flooding and the walls and roofs from caving in. As a result, coal prices fell steadily, plunging from $3.75 a ton in 1920 to $1.31 in 1932. Labor costs made up about 60 percent of the price of coal at the mine. As prices fell, the operators searched desperately for ways of cutting labor costs. When the union defended miners' wages, the operators angrily or in desperation attacked the union.

At times the industry was capable of producing 50 percent more coal than it actually dug—700 million tons or more, when the country was burning 500 million or less. The industry's huge capacity helped to push prices steadily downward, in turn putting still greater pressure on the miners' pay. At the same time, coal was falling back in the contest to provide the nation's energy. Coal supplied 84 percent of it in 1920, 79 percent in 1925, and only 73 percent in 1930. The nation used a steadily increasing volume of energy, but oil, natural gas, and hydroelectric power captured the lion's share of the increase.

The miner's labor, too, became more productive. The average miner dug 3.5 tons of coal a day in 1890. By 1931, he turned out 5.3 tons a day. The nation's coal supply could be dug in about three and a half days a week. That meant that the average miner had to keep himself and his family a full week on a half week's pay, or that the coal supply could be dug with half or less of the work force. The combination of falling prices, relentless downward pressure on wages, and short-time work added up to ugly, grinding, hopeless poverty for countless thousands of miners and their families. Depression cut production, forced prices down, and slashed the number of men working in the mines still further. "No region and relatively few firms," one observer noted, "managed to escape the disaster."

The UMW had once supported government ownership of the mines as the cure for the industry's sickness. It coupled that proposal with an insistence that the miners be guaranteed "the free and unrestricted right to organize and bargain collectively." Lewis, then climbing to union power, endorsed the policy and made it an issue in his race against Gompers in 1921. He told a Congressional committee that year: "If private industry cannot . . . regularize employment and stabilize output, it may be necessary for the Government to assume the burden." Brophy, the union's leading advocate of nationalization, agreed but he didn't think Lewis meant it.

By 1925, Lewis made it clear that he had no sympathy with government ownership. He swung to the opposite pole in a book entitled *The Miners' Fight for American Standards*. ("Would that mine enemy hath written a book," Lewis complained some years later.) He denounced government controls—they would paralyze "initiative and enterprise." Instead, he urged the "free play" of "natural economic laws" regulated only by supply and demand.

Even more vigorously, he argued for an industry-wide high-wage policy. High wages would provide a decent living standard for miners and help to maintain general prosperity by sustaining purchasing power. They would force high-cost mines out of business, make out-of-date equipment and incompetent management too expensive. Wage reductions, he contended, brought distress to the masses and bankruptcy to business. High wages, he said, are "in unison with the heartbeats of America . . . the very essence of the American spirit."

Labor relations in the industry, Lewis went on, must be based on peace, not strife. He added, "The American Constitution must mean what it says in every coal field in America.

"American law must run to the remotest corner of America."

In the spring of 1929, a Senate subcommittee toured coal fields in central and western Pennsylvania. It found, the *Journal* reported, "starvation, poverty, suffering, brutality, disregard for law, utter contempt for all human considerations. It found that these coal companies had brazenly broken their contracts with the United Mine Workers of America; reduced wages; evicted thousands of families from their homes; hired hundreds of armed thugs to intimidate, browbeat, and terrorize the union miners who refused to accept the new conditions; imported thousands of undesirable riff-raff strikebreakers from the slums of the great cities and from the cotton fields of the South." Years of depression underscored the industry's tragic plight.

The large coal interests, the Mellons and the Rockefellers, were asked for their answers to the industry's problems. They had none. The United Mine Workers, however, now proposed government regulation, coupled with legal recognition of labor's right to organize and bargain collectively. The Watson bill embodying the UMW proposal and its successors died of Congressional indifference.

By then, not merely the coal industry but the nation's entire economy was sick. Senator Robert La Follette called for proposals to end the depression. Lewis responded with a national variation of his coal-industry plan. He proposed a national economic council to "plan" the economy's future. He urged a six-hour day, a five-day week to put the jobless back to work. He wanted to eliminate the manufacturer who survived only by paying pauper wages and selling at cutthroat prices. He suggested freeing industry from antitrust laws, letting it agree on price and production controls. At the same time, the government must give labor an "ironclad guarantee" of its rights.

This was another Lewis. Under the pressures of un-ending economic warfare in the coal industry, of the depression and its suffering, of the attrition of his own union, Lewis's ideas had changed. The "free play" of "natural economic laws" of only a few years before was forgotten. Now he urged strong and decisive inter-vention by the Federal Government into the economy in general and into the coal industry in particular.

Lewis supported the Republican candidate for pres-ident in 1932 as he had in previous elections. Vice Pres-ident Murray and Secretary-Treasurer Kennedy jour-neyed to Hyde Park to meet Franklin Delano Roosevelt. Murray reported that they liked what they saw; they would support FDR.

The *Journal* paid little attention to the campaign, scarcely more to Roosevelt's victory. Shortly before his inauguration, it commented, "As yet, no one seems to know anything about what policies Roosevelt will adopt. . . . The people are wondering . . . hoping and pray-ing. . . ."

Recovery and Reorganization

"Thank God for President Roosevelt and
President Lewis"

The miners' hope, Lewis was convinced, lay in Federal
regulation. "A conspiracy of mismanagement," he
charged, had laid waste all that the union had tried to
do. Despite the desperate needs of the miners and of
the industry, Lewis said the union would seek no special
legislation. Instead it would support efforts to write
laws to help end the general depression.

Economic recovery was at the top of the Roosevelt Administration's list. Lewis became deeply involved
in drafting legislation to bring it about. He led a fight
to include labor's right to organize and bargain collectively in any general legislation aimed at restoring prosperity. Five times, the legislative draftsmen threw out
the guarantee. Each time, *Fortune* reported, Lewis glow-
ered and forced it back—the last time over President
Roosevelt's doubts. If industry was to be given the
power to drive out the price cutter and the "chiseler,"
Lewis insisted that labor be given equal power to drive
out pauper wages and sweatshop conditions. The guarantee was written into the final bill as Section 7a.

The bill itself, the National Industrial Recovery Act,

set up the National Recovery Administration (NRA) to guide industry in establishing codes of fair competition. The codes would establish procedures for regulating prices, production, and competitive practices for each industry. The codes would also fix minimum wages, maximum hours of work, and apply the guarantees of Section 7a. NRA's goals, President Roosevelt declared, were "a reasonable profit for industry and living wages for labor."

Earlier that year, Lewis had called the miners to a special meeting. He planned, he told them, to spend every last penny in the union treasury in a massive organizing campaign. Every member of the union's field forces and all the volunteers they could recruit would be mobilized to carry the union message into every coal field in the nation. The guarantees of what became Section 7a would serve, Lewis said, as a "declaration of independence" for miners everywhere.

Now, union organizers made their way up roads that gunmen had barred for years into coal fields where they had long been absent. Union signs broke out on mine tipples, and organizing fires brightened the nights in the hollows of West Virginia and Kentucky hills. "The President wants you to unionize," the union leaflets shouted. "Here is your union. Never mind about the dues now. Just join up." Miners sang:

> In nineteen hundred an' thirty-three
> When Mr. Roosevelt took his seat,
> He said to President John L. Lewis
> In union we must be.

Long-dormant local unions sprang to life. New locals were created overnight. "A Tidal Wave," the *Journal* shouted. Central Pennsylvania signed up, with the Pittsburgh district close behind. Connellsville and Westmoreland counties were unionized for the first time since the ill-fated strike of 1922. West Virginia joined the union, including Mingo and Logan counties and the Hitchman mine, where the yellow-dog contract had been hung around the union's neck. Harlan county in Kentucky turned union.

President Roosevelt signed the National Industrial Recovery Act into law on June 15, 1933. By then, Lewis boasted, 135,000 bituminous miners had joined the union. "The handwriting is on the wall," Lewis challenged the operators. "Eighteen million stomachs clash against backbones." Some twenty-five different versions of a bituminous-coal code were proposed. It was finally written by General Hugh Johnson, the stentorian-voiced, table-thumping head of NRA.

President Roosevelt suggested a union contract to undergird the coal code. General Johnson promptly brought the union and operators together. The contract that was produced nearly two months later set a basic $5 a day wage in mines north of the Ohio river, $4.60 south of the river. (At the time, a third of the nation's mines were paying less than $3.50 a day. Weekly earnings ranged from $6 to $10.) The contract set a forty-hour week, allowed the union to select its own checkweighmen, and established a 2,000-pound ton (instead of the 2,200- and 2,400-pound tons enforced

"Here She Comes!"

June 15, 1933. *United Mine Workers of America*

by operators at their tipples). Company scrip and token money of any kind were outlawed. Miners would no longer be compelled to live in company houses or to trade at company stores. The contract covered well over 300,000 miners—"the greatest in magnitude and importance that has ever been negotiated in the history of collective bargaining in the United States," a joint union-operator statement declared.

Across the land, other depression-ridden workers rose to the challenge of Section 7a. By the thousands—rubber workers in Akron, auto workers in Detroit, steel workers along the Monongahela, workers in lumber and sawmills, in cement and aluminum and textiles—they crowded into old unions or organized new ones. The Ladies' Garment Workers and the Amalgamated Clothing Workers launched sweeping organizing drives. Hundreds of thousands—hosiery workers and silk workers, dressmakers and shoemakers, steel workers, tool-and-die makers, cotton pickers—walked out on strike, in all, three times as many as had been involved in strikes the year before.

Lewis offered to put a big part of the Mine Workers' treasury at the disposal of the AFL if William Green would agree to spend it on an intensive organizing drive. The AFL unions, Lewis said, ". . . were gasping for breath to stay alive."

Green was reluctant. "Now, John," Lewis quoted Green as saying, "let's take it easy."

In August, 1933, some 70,000 miners in Pennsylvania went on strike at the H. C. Frick Coal Company mines, part of the powerful nonunion empire of the U. S. Steel Corporation. Along with other steel companies operating coal mines, the Frick company refused to apply the conditions of the bituminous-coal code to its "captive" mines. Nor would it deal with the union. President Roosevelt and General Johnson planted themselves be-

tween the warring parties and negotiated an understanding. The captive-mine owners would maintain the
wages and conditions of the Appalachian union contract, and the National Labor Board would hold elections among the miners to choose bargaining representatives. In the final count, UMW representatives were
chosen at nineteen mines, nonunion representatives at
eight. Soon after, the Frick company signed agreements
with the bargaining representatives (but withheld formal recognition of the union).

When the officers of the UMW mounted the platform to open the union's 34th convention in January,
1934, they were given a tumultuous reception. Lewis
exulted, "Delegates from every coal field on the Northern American continent north of the mines of Mexico
are present at this convention," he said, "greater progress, may I say with pardonable pride, than has been
made by any other trade union organization in America."
And this, he went on, despite those who had opposed
the union's policies, proclaiming "the lack of virtue in
its representatives."

The NRA honeymoon, such as it was, however, was
nearing the end. Lewis soon warned that operators were
violating the code and renewing the old competitive
warfare. "Deliberate wrecking" of the code's prices
threatened the union's wages, he asserted; they "cannot
be sacrificed to any such policy of monumental stupidity."

Against this possibility, Lewis moved to obtain
stronger protection. Senator Joseph Guffey of Pennsylvania introduced a bill creating a National Bituminous

Commission to regulate coal prices and production. Like the earlier versions of Federal coal legislation and the NRA, itself, it included Section 7a's guarantees to workers.

"I speak not for the dollars invested," Lewis told the House Labor Committee, while urging adoption of the Guffey bill. "I speak not for the inanimate tons of coal; I speak for the human beings who go down into these coal mines and serve the public interest by getting the coal. . . . The men I represent, during this thirty-seven year period, have carried out of these mines, on stretchers, seventy-nine thousand dead men.

". . . . Just a couple of Christmases ago," Lewis continued, "on Christmas Eve, I went to the scene of an explosion in Illinois that killed all the men in the mine. It was not a large mine, but an ancient, old, high-cost, uneconomic mine . . . and the men were trying vainly to continue in operation against competition that they could not meet. They had no timber in it, they had no air in it; they had gas in it . . . and it blew up. And for a Christmas Eve gift, the families of that community gathered around that pit head, waiting for their dead to be brought out of that mine."

That summer, the United States Supreme Court ruled the NRA unconstitutional. Its ruling killed the coal code, along with all the other industry codes. The legal guarantee of labor's rights died with them. At that moment, too, the Appalachian Bituminous Wage Conference broke up. No miners would work after June 16, the union announced. This is no strike, the *Journal* explained.

"It is a suspension of work by the miners because they have no contract determining their wages." At FDR's request, the strike deadline was repeatedly delayed. Finally, the Guffey bill was passed; soon after, the miners and operators signed a new contract. It raised the miners' pay 50 cents a day to $5.50 in the North, $5.10 in the South. "Thank God," a miner wrote, "for President Roosevelt and President Lewis."

As it turned out, the Guffey Act was also declared unconstitutional. It was promptly replaced by a second, written to skirt the hurdles set up by the Court's decision. The first act had barely had time to get into operation; the second had only a little more. The tempo of the economy was rising. The national defense program —later war itself—made its minimum prices unnecessary. The NRA, glowingly hailed at the outset and roundly cussed and discussed during its two hectic years of life, faded from the scene. The miners, the clothing workers, the ladies' garment workers, a few other unions had taken full advantage of the brief opportunity. They had gained hundreds of thousands of new members, new contracts, better conditions. But many of the new unions evaporated; many of the new union members melted away.

In his own union, Lewis was master of a far more powerful force than anyone would have dared guess a short time before. The union's resources climbed from a few thousand dollars to millions. For the first time since he took office, Lewis had no serious internal opposition. He could turn to other problems. These stretched from the encirclement of his miners by the wealthy, powerful, and antiunion steel industry, to the lack of effective organization among millions of the nation's workers, and to the reluctance and timidity of the labor movement. Solution of these problems soon became his all-absorbing task.

12 /

The CIO Is Formed

"That wild blow . . . echoed in every
union hall across the land"

To countless thousands of workers, Section 7a proved
to be worthless. NRA was timid and reluctant to enforce their rights. Employers fired them with impunity
when they joined unions. Their leaders were frequently
new and unschooled, or old and fearful. Often their
strikes were settled under government pressure, leaving them little to show for their pains. Auto workers
were discouraged and divided. The traditional union
of steel workers hesitated to move against the giant
steel corporations. "You can't fight a two-billion dollar
diversified corporation," its tired, old leader declared.
Textile workers struck, but their union was denied
recognition and the strikers were blacklisted. Millions
of workers signed up in unions, then dropped out.

Though business picked up speed and employment
increased, joblessness remained high. The unemployed,
who had numbered over 13 million (at least) in 1933,
fell to 10.6 million in 1935, 9 million in 1936—high by
any measure. Still, when employers balked at union recognition or refused to raise wages or cut hours, millions
of workers took to the picket lines. Their growing pro-

tests dwarfed the strike wave of 1933, and violence flared from one end of the country to the other.

In the spring of 1933—April or May, as he remembered it—Lewis had urged William Green to launch a massive organizing campaign. Green objected that the Federation did not have the money. He doubted, too, whether AFL craft unions could effectively organize these millions of semiskilled industrial workers. Remembering the event later, Lewis said he knew that night that the AFL would never organize the nation's basic industries.

The United Mine Workers had long stood in the AFL for industrial unions: single unions covering all the workers, skilled and unskilled alike, in an entire industry. Eugene V. Debs had dramatized the idea in his American Railway Union; Socialists and other radicals had made industrial unions an article of their faith. But the AFL had become, over the years, the domain of a handful of unions representing skilled craftsmen.

In the beginning, in 1881, Sam Gompers had told the founding convention, "We do not want to exclude any working man who believes in and belongs to organized labor." Under the young Gompers, the AFL organized unions of many kinds of workers, unskilled and semiskilled as well as skilled. In 1902, in the Scranton Declaration, the Federation gave the UMW an industrial union charter taking in workers of every skill in the coal industry. At the same time, it reaffirmed the jurisdictional territories carved out elsewhere by the craft unions. These—the building trades, metal trades, printing trades, virtually all unions of skilled craftsmen—gave the AFL its dominant direction, its philosophy, its program. Gompers in time became their prisoner. He came to reflect the craft-union philosophy ably and effectively, giving up or drastically modifying the broader beliefs of his younger years. Green, though he had been raised in the industrial-union faith of the UMW, was also their captive. Now, as workers in countless industries cried out for organization, the issue of craft versus industrial unions was debated with rising heat.

Union-hungry workers flooding into the Federation were temporarily placed in so-called federal locals. The metal-trades union, led by John P. Frey, demanded that the new unionists be turned over at once to their respective crafts. Others, however, called for organizing them into new industrial unions. The 1933 convention of the AFL upheld the craft unions, but it also agreed that organizing workers in mass-production industries raised special problems.

To consider some of these problems, the representatives of seventy-five national and international unions—the UMW was absent—met in a conference in January, 1934. The conference declared that the basic principle of craft unionism on which the AFL was founded could not be altered. Unions could organize in whatever form seemed best, it said, as long as they did not poach on the "rights" of the craft unions.

To their own convention, the UMW officers made their position clear. The UMW hoped the Federation would agree on plant or industry unions in the mass-production industries. The UMW had no intention of interfering with existing unions, but it seemed "reasonable" that there should be room in the AFL for other industrial unions like the Mine Workers. It was the only way, the report declared, collective bargaining could be established in basic industries.

Lewis underscored the point. "Every year," he said on one occasion, "the coal operators would begin by denying my people a rise in wages . . . by citing the lower wage of the unorganized steel workers. . . . Since the mine workers were earning more money than the steel workers, we should be satisfied." It was "a simple, elementary economic fact," Lewis insisted, that the steel workers' low pay was a drag on the miners' wages. "The mine workers could never really win a just wage until the steel workers were organized and their miserable wages raised to a human, decent standard."

Lewis went to the 1934 AFL convention at San Francisco determined to establish industrial unions in the nation's mass-production industries. In the Resolutions Committee, he, on the one hand, and Matthew Woll, veteran chief of the photo engravers, on the other, battled for six days. They finally emerged with a compromise resolution, recognizing that new conditions existed in mass-production industries. It ordered the Executive Council to charter industrial unions in the auto, cement, aluminum, and other mass-production industries as might be necessary. It called for an early organizing campaign in the iron and steel industry.

Then the resolution added that the rights of craft unions would be protected. They would be given every opportunity to recruit workers on jobs coming under their jurisdiction. The job of resolving the obvious conflict between craft-union rights and the proposed industrial-union charters was left with the Executive Council.

Early in 1935, the Executive Council tackled the problem. Lewis urged an immediate industrial charter for the auto workers. Green concurred; they must be organized ". . . en masse. We cannot separate them." But the council separated them. It authorized an industrial charter but carved out some of the skilled workers. Green warned, "The moment you attempt to segregate them you will never get anywhere." He added, "I know we will fail." A similarly bobtailed charter was authorized for the rubber workers. Ambitious unions in other mass-production industries were denied even that much.

When it came to the steel industry, Michael F. Tighe, the aging and conservative president of the feeble Amalgamated Association of Iron, Steel and Tin Workers, asked for 200,000 dollars for an organizing drive. He added that he was convinced the plants could be organized only industrially. President Green agreed it was the only way these workers could deal with the powerful steel companies. He added that workers might be transferred to other unions later, but now, "the difficulties are too great." Arthur P. Wharton, head of the International Association of Machinists, balked. He suggested that the Federation form a joint council of craft unions to carry on the campaign. Lewis argued that the San Francisco convention had authorized a change in tactics. Under Wharton's views it would never be tried. The Executive

Council finally voted to invite all unions claiming jurisdiction over steel workers to take part in a joint campaign.

On a bright summer Sunday soon afterward, Lewis
invited a number of his associates in the United Mine
Workers to breakfast. The group sat long over the coffee,
Lewis talking in a rambling way about the state of the
labor movement. Millions of workers were unorganized,
he said, often existing in "a condition of virtual serfdom,"
their helplessness "a cancer draining upon the well-being
of others." He compared the steel industry to "feudal
baronies where the only American institution that sur-
vives and functions in an American manner is the postage
stamp." He no longer expected the AFL to live up to the
San Francisco resolution. "I think," he summed up, "that
the United Mine Workers of America are sufficiently
secure to try and do something about it."

At that moment, another development of high importance was also coming to a head. The NRA's National
Labor Board had relied heavily on the prestige of its
members and public sentiment to enforce Section 7a.
Employers, however, had defied the law and the Board
without penalty. In 1934, and again in 1935, Senator
Robert Wagner of New York, who had headed the Board,
introduced a labor-disputes bill. His bill became even
more important when the Supreme Court killed Section
7a.

Wagner's bill proposed to write into the nation's law
a basic guarantee of the worker's right to join a union and
bargain collectively. Interference with that right or re-

fusal of an employer to bargain collectively would constitute an unfair labor practice. To remedy—and to prevent—unfair labor practices, the act would create the
National Labor Relations Board (NLRB). The Board
would also conduct secret-ballot elections to allow workers a free choice of bargaining representatives. President
Roosevelt signed the Wagner Act into law on July 27,
1935, calling it "an act of common justice."

A committee of lawyers, organized by the influential
American Liberty League and representing many of the
nation's most powerful industrialists, called it "an illegal
interference with the individual freedom of employees."
In a 132-page brief, the committee unhesitatingly called
the Act unconstitutional. A good many employers, both
large and small, gave the committee's opinion unusual
weight, acting often as if it were, in fact, the law. As it
turned out, the opinion was wrong. In 1937, the Supreme
Court affirmed the constitutionality of the Wagner Act.

The Wagner Act marked a drastic change in the nation's and the labor movement's attitudes toward the
Government and its place in labor-management relations.
Unions had long resisted Government interference in
their affairs. They had bitterly protested invasion of their
activities by the courts until the Norris-La Guardia Act
of 1932 gave them sanctuary from antiunion injunctions.
They had rejected labor and social legislation (minimum
wages and unemployment insurance, for example) rather
than accept even limited Government control. But now,
the Wagner Act wrote into the nation's law the worker's
right to "self-organization . . . to engage in concerted

activities for the purpose of collective bargaining, or other mutual aid and protection." It provided governmental machinery to enforce it. It was a massive and decisive intervention that radically changed the course of the nation's labor relations and of the trade-union movement.

Lewis had his own plans for changing the course of the labor movement. He marched on Atlantic City, the AFL convention city in 1935, one observer reported, "like a general." Twenty-one resolutions touching on the industrial-union question faced the convention. Unable to reach a new compromise, the Resolutions Committee brought out both majority and minority reports. Powerful figures lined up on both sides. Woll at one time had been considered Gompers's "crown prince." John P. Frey carried the formidable weight of the metal-trades craft unions. Wharton of the Machinists, Hutcheson of the Carpenters, Victor Olander of the Seamen, Tobin of the Teamsters backed the craft-union stand. Lewis had the backing of Charles P. Howard of the Typographical Union, David Dubinsky of the Ladies' Garment Workers, Sidney Hillman of the Clothing Workers, among many.

The majority report supported the San Francisco policy. The Council had attempted, in good faith, to carry it out, it said; the opponents either did not understand it or they were simply seeking to set it aside.

The minority report pointed out that the AFL had clearly failed to establish unions in mass-production industries. In industries where the jobs fell under more than one union or under no union at all, it argued, "the only form that will be acceptable to the workers or adequately meet their needs" is industrial organization. Cutting out small groups of workers in answer to jurisdictional claims made workers afraid that they would be divided into small, powerless groups. The minority report urged that they allow these workers to organize without fear that their unity would be broken by the craft unions.

Frey argued that the charters granted the craft unions by the AFL were binding contracts; they could not be set aside without the consent of both parties. Wharton told the delegates that twenty-one railroad crafts had survived six years of depression with memberships intact through a plan of cooperation. Industrial-union supporters, on the other hand, underscored the failure of the Federation to organize the unorganized. Lewis ticked off the case for the minority report in a towering speech.

A year before, he recalled, for six days and almost six nights, the Resolutions Committee had wrestled with the problem. Its final report called for industrial-union charters in mass-production industries. "What happened?" he asked. The charter finally issued in the auto industry was practically limited to the men on the assembly line. He could no longer put much faith in the Executive Council's "fair words."

The craft unions, he argued, could show only twenty-five years of constant, unbroken failure. The unions of recent years were "dying like the grass withering before the autumn sun." The miners' struggle was made harder because the AFL had not organized the steel industry.

The dream of the future of millions of Americans was involved, Lewis stressed. The AFL had no right to turn away from them. "Strong men do not remain strong," he reminded the delegates. The time might come when they would be unable to "withstand the lightning and the gale.

"Now prepare yourself," he pleaded, "by making a contribution to your less fortunate brethren, heed this cry . . . that comes from the hearts of men. Organize the unorganized! And in so doing make the American Federation of Labor the greatest instrumentality that has ever been forged in the history of modern civilization to befriend the cause of humanity and champion human rights."

The industrial-union report was defeated, but the question kept recurring. Delegates from rubber, radio, mine, and mill kept urging a new policy. Their way was blocked, though, not least by the towering figure of Big Bill Hutcheson, powerful head of the Carpenters' Union. Hutcheson and Lewis had always held similar views and frequently worked together. Like Lewis, Hutcheson was a big man, 6 feet tall and 220 pounds. When a delegate raised the question of industrial unionism in the rubber plants, Hutcheson raised a point of order. The question had already been settled, he contended. Lewis objected; the delegate should be heard on a problem facing his own union. "This thing of raising points of order," he added, "is rather small potatoes."

"I was raised on small potatoes," Hutcheson replied.

As Lewis returned to his seat he paused to tell Hutcheson that his opposition was pretty small stuff. "We could have made you small," was the reply. "We could have kept you off the Executive Council, you crazy bastard."

Lewis swung a wild haymaker. It caught Hutcheson on the jaw; the two men grappled, crashed against a table, and fell awkwardly to the floor. President Green wildly hammered his gavel as delegates tried to separate the two heavyweights.

Years later, Saul Alinsky asked Lewis if his blow had been planned. Lewis replied, "Bill Hutcheson represented symbolically the kind of leadership in the American Federation of Labor that the workers of this country detested. It was Bill Hutcheson's supporters and associates . . . who successfully blocked every single move that was made in the direction of industrial unionism. All I will say is that I never walked an aisle so slowly and grimly as I did that day in the 1935 convention."

Lewis's target was larger than Hutcheson's jaw. He wanted, the labor movement needed, he told Alinsky, "an act of some kind, an act dramatic to the degree that it would inspire and enthuse the workers of this country." The crunch of his wild blow echoed in every union hall across the land.

Rivalry between the AFL and the CIO

"If that be treason, let Mr. Green make the most of it"

On the last day of the AFL's 1935 convention, Lewis met a small group of union leaders in the dining room of an Atlantic City hotel. Among those at the table were Sidney Hillman of the Clothing Workers, David Dubinsky of the Ladies' Garment Workers, Charles P. Howard of the Typographical Union, Thomas H. Brown of the Mill, Mine and Smelter Workers. For some time, they talked about carrying on the fight for industrial organization. They agreed to meet again in Washington.

At the Washington meeting on November 9, they set up a committee with Lewis as chairman, Howard as secretary. The Atlantic City group was joined by Harvey C. Freming of the Oil Workers, Max Zaritsky of the United Hatters, Thomas P. McMahon of the Textile Workers. John Brophy, now reconciled with Lewis, was made director. He and Howard prepared a press release announcing the formation of the Committee for Industrial Organization (CIO). The Committee, the announcement said, would encourage and promote the organization of unorganized workers in mass-production and other industries on an industrial basis "under the banner of the American Federation of Labor."

This was a time, as Walter Reuther, later president of the Auto Workers, recalled it, when "injustice was as commonplace as streetcars. When men walked into their jobs, they left their dignity, their citizenship and their humanity outside. They were required to report for work whether there was work or not. While they waited on the convenience of supervisors and foremen they were unpaid. They could be fired without the necessity for a pretext. They were subjected to arbitrary, senseless rules —no smoking, no eating, no resting. Men were tortured by regulations that made difficult even going to the toilet. . . . Men were fired to make way for supervisors' nephews, foremen's brothers-in-law, college chums. Long years of employment entitled workers to nothing. When men slowed down at forty or forty-five they were laid off without hope of recall. After layoffs there was never any assurance that a man would get his job back if work started up again, or if he did get his job that he would return at his old pay. The millions of unemployed outside the plant gates were used to frighten workers into subservience. . . . There was no one and no agency to which a worker could appeal."

Lewis offered workers just that "agency" in the CIO. In radio talks he defined its goals. The nation's industries, he declared, could produce "an abundant life" for all of the people. The capacity to produce would have no outlet, though, unless consumers were given a greater capacity to consume—widespread employment, increased wages, more leisure. The workers in mass-production industries, he asserted, must be able to support their families "under conditions of health, decency and comfort, to own their own home, to educate their children."

Opposition was not long in coming. Wharton of the Machinists swore that he "would rather see the labor movement go under and myself in hell than have John L. Lewis get away with it." Hutcheson called for immediate expulsion of the CIO unions. On November 23, Green wrote Lewis, voicing his fears that formation of the Committee, however "laudable" its purpose, would lead to strife and bitterness. Affiliated unions, Green argued, were bound by the majority decisions of the AFL conventions. He urged prompt dissolution of the CIO.

Lewis penned a hasty reply. "Effective this date, I resign as vice president of the American Federation of Labor." He explained his action to a jammed press conference. He disagreed with the AFL's organizing policy, he said. It had failed to bring the great mass of workers into the organized-labor movement. Great numbers of workers were ready to join, but they would not submit to being divided up into small groups and handed out among the craft unions. The CIO, he declared, would promote industrial unionism in a vigorous campaign. To his astonished associates, he explained further that he had acted abruptly, without consulting them, "to dramatize what the Committee is trying to do."

Secretary Howard wrote a more considered reply. He assured Green of the loyalty of the Committee members. The Committee had no intention of raiding established unions. Its only purpose was to organize and bargain collectively where no union now existed and to inform rank-and-file union members of its viewpoint.

Lewis added several paragraphs to Howard's letter.

He suggested that Green's "private sympathies and individual inclinations" were with industrial unionism, while "your official actions and public utterances will be in support of its adversaries." He invited Green to "return to your father's house. You will be welcome." Lewis offered to step aside to make a place for him.

Green replied bluntly that he was in his "father's house," and intended to stay there.

Soon afterwards, though, Green returned to his "father's house"—the convention of the Mine Workers—fresh from a meeting of the AFL Executive Council. Some Council members had wanted to suspend the unions in the CIO immediately. Green had told the Council that it had no authority to suspend an international union. Only a convention could suspend or revoke a union's charter. The Executive Council contented itself with a formal demand that the CIO dissolve itself at once.

That was the message Green carried to the miners. For two hours he pleaded the Executive Council's case. Lewis had already made his attitude clear: Unless the convention ordered him to do so, he had told the delegates, "all the members of the Executive Council . . . will be wearing asbestos suits in hell before that committee is dissolved."

When Green ended his lengthy appeal, Lewis asked delegates who had changed their minds to stand. "The chair sees two delegates," he intoned.

"Again the question recurs upon the fiat of the Executive Council . . . read to this convention as an ultimatum by President Green. It demands that the president of the United Mine Workers of America, with his associates on the Committee for Industrial Organization, like quarry slaves at night, scourged to their dungeon, dissolve, disband, cease and desist. . . . Let those delegates . . . who believe that the president of the United Mine Workers of America should comply with that request rise to their feet.

"The chair sees one delegate arise. . . ."

Lewis turned to the defeated and humiliated Green.

"President Green, you have received the answer of the United Mine Workers of America to your ultimatum."

The Federation, nevertheless, again called on the CIO to dissolve. The CIO was not interested. The auto workers and rubber workers had recently affiliated. An industrial union of electrical, radio, and machine workers, rebuffed by the 1935 AFL convention, was being formed. It had signed an agreement for an organizing campaign in steel.

The Executive Council was told that Lewis was prepared to dissolve the CIO if the AFL would agree to organize certain basic industries on an industrial-union basis. But the Executive Council would wait no longer. It ordered the CIO unions suspended.

"An appalling blunder," Lewis commented, "an act of incredible and crass stupidity." Later, he added, "The only crime of which we are accused is an attempt to organize workers and make them members of the American Federation of Labor. If that be treason, let Mr. Green make the most of it."

Across the country, local labor groups of every kind protested the Executive Council action. Many supported the CIO; others thought simply that the issue should

Going Strong!

February 15, 1936. *United Mine Workers of America*

have been left to the upcoming AFL convention. Now the convention, with the suspended unions absent, quickly and overwhelmingly affirmed the Executive Council's action.

In apparent retaliation, the Executive Board of the

Mine Workers accused Green, its former secretary-treasurer, of associating with "avowed enemies" of the union, of conspiring to suspend the Mine Workers from the AFL, of distorting its aims and objectives. Green replied that the long record of his service to the UMW was denial enough of the charges.

Alongside the AFL-CIO battle, workers were fighting an even fiercer and often bloody battle for union recognition and collective bargaining rights. The industrial warfare reached an explosive climax in the auto workers' sitdown at General Motors.

14 /
The Auto Workers' Sitdown

"It broke the back of antiunionism"

Early in 1936, the CIO swung into action. It sent help to the struggling auto workers and dispatched organizers and money to the rubber workers. Lewis took a hand in electrical workers' negotiations (facing his former NRA associate, General Johnson). Walkouts, sitdowns, unrest spread across the country. Workers were tired, Lewis said, of waiting for industry to "alleviate their social agony."

At Akron, rubber workers sat down in the plants, demanding recognition of their union. A miner working as a CIO organizer was puzzled. "They just stand there doing nothing all day. The straw bosses is nuts and I don't know what to make of it either." After six weeks, Goodyear recognized the United Rubber Workers—the CIO's first victory.

The sitdown strike came as a surprise to many, but it was not new. The Wobblies (Industrial Workers of the World) had made dramatic use of the slowdown, the folded-arm strike, the stay-in. French factory workers, Yugoslav and Polish coal miners, and Spanish copper miners had used the stay-in technique. Rubber workers made the first major use of it in this country in the thirties.

Employers complained that the sitdown strike robbed them of the use of their private property and accused sitdowners of every crime from simple trespass to general insurrection. Supporters theorized that the worker was entitled to use "such orderly methods as may force the employer to meet his representatives in collective bargaining." Others suggested that the employers themselves had shown the way by housing strikebreakers in their plants to resume production. It didn't seem right, President Roosevelt told Secretary of Labor Frances Perkins, to shoot and kill a lot of people just because they wouldn't get off your property. Lewis suggested that a CIO contract "is adequate protection for any employer against sitdowns, liedowns, or any other kind of strike." William Green would have nothing to do with the sitdown, "personally and officially."

Workers liked the sitdown strike because it required only minimum picket lines, often none at all, and accordingly reduced the danger that they would have their heads cracked by police or strikebreakers or professional guards. The employers' buildings, machinery, and materials offered both a shield of safety and handy, if unusual, weapons against being forcibly removed. The sitdown halted production quickly and effectively and prevented strikebreakers from filling strikers' jobs.

In 1939, the United States Supreme Court ruled that the sitdown was "an illegal seizure." Before then, however, the CIO made it a major weapon in its organizing offensive—nowhere with greater effect than in the nation's auto plants. John Brophy, new director of the CIO, had found the auto workers "worried, frustrated and resentful." The AFL had denied them an industrial charter, attempting to strip them of the skilled mechanics. The La Follette Committee revealed that General Motors had spent close to a million dollars to spy on them. In Michigan, a court held the Wagner Act unconstitutional. A state court ruled picketing illegal. GM obtained a court order preventing the National Labor Relations Board from intervening in a dispute in its St. Louis plant.

In mid-December, 1936, Lewis called on General Motors to sit down and talk out the auto workers' problems. "Collective bargaining is the law of the land," he reminded GM, "and we think General Motors should now do a little collective bargaining." When the union asked for a meeting, William Knudsen, GM's executive vice president, arranged "a personal interview," making it plain that this did not constitute, in any way, recognition of the union. If the workers had complaints, he insisted, the complaints should be taken up with the plant managers. "That's not collective bargaining," Lewis growled. "That's just evasion."

On December 28, the men in GM's Fisher Body plant at Cleveland sat down. The UAW announced that the strike could be ended only as part of a national settlement. Four more plants were shut down by sitdowns in the next two days, seven more on New Year's Day, 1937. "The CIO stands squarely behind these sitdowns," Lewis declared.

GM would not consider negotiations until the men left the plants, Knudsen announced. Sitdown strikers are clearly trespassers and violators of the law of the land, he said. In any case, a national agreement was unthinkable. More sitdowns swept GM plants. The company obtained an injunction ordering the men to leave the plants. The order was invalidated, however, when the union revealed that the judge who wrote it owned more than a quarter of a million dollars of General Motors stock.

At Flint, Michigan, police and sitdowners clashed in a daylong battle of tear gas and gunfire against car-door hinges and fire hoses. The next day, Governor Frank Murphy of Michigan arranged a truce; the strikers would evacuate the plants, and negotiations would begin at once. To the thump of brass bands and with colors flying, strikers marched out of the Cadillac and Fleetwood plants. Other sitdowners prepared to leave. Then a reporter told UAW officials that General Motors had also agreed to negotiate with the Flint Alliance. The Alliance had been organized by a onetime Buick employee. Its avowed purpose was to clear the way for nonunion men to return to work. The strikers saw it as a company-sponsored, antiunion effort to break their strike. Crying "double-cross," they halted the evacuation and trooped back into the plants.

Secretary of Labor Perkins persuaded GM President Alfred Sloan and Knudsen to meet with her in Washington, though they stubbornly refused to talk to Lewis. Fuming, Lewis turned to the man in the White House.

"For six months during the [1936] presidential campaign the economic royalists represented by General Motors and the DuPonts contributed their money and used their energy to drive this Administration from power," he reminded President Roosevelt. "The Administration asked labor to help repel this attack and labor gave it. The same economic royalists now have their fangs in labor. The workers of this country expect the Administration to help the strikers in every reasonable way."

In a deliberate rebuke, FDR commented that it was no time for headlines. Sloan read Lewis's statement in the papers and angrily departed for New York. In an apparent attempt to balance his reprimands, FDR called Sloan's action "a very unfortunate decision." To Secretary Perkins, the President complained, "Why can't these fellows in General Motors meet with the committee of workers? Talk it all out? They would get a settlement. It wouldn't be so terrible."

At Flint, union members sat down in Chevy Plant Number 4. The next day, GM obtained a new injunction ordering strikers to leave the plants. The Flint chief of police warned Lewis to call off his union men. "The good citizens of Flint are getting pretty nearly out of hand." The sheriff appealed to Governor Murphy for help. The sitdowners sent the Governor a telegram: ". . . we have decided to stay in the plant. We have no illusions about the sacrifice that this decision will entail . . . many of us will be killed and we take this means of making it known to our wives, to our children, to the people of the State of Michigan and the country, that if this result follows from the attempt to eject us, you are the one who must be held responsible for our deaths!"

With President Roosevelt's help, the Governor brought Lewis and Knudsen together. On Lewis's arrival in Detroit, the Governor formally demanded that strikers evacuate the plants. Lewis told the Governor that he did not doubt his ability to call out the soldiers and "shoot the members of our union out of those plants," but if the order were issued, he added, "I shall enter one of those plants with my own people. And the militia will have the pleasure of shooting me out of the plants with them."

For eight tense days, Murphy held the negotiators in session. Tension mounted. State troops were reinforced. Union men flooded into town. The judge who wrote the eviction order commanded the sheriff to carry it out. But Governor Murphy persisted and finally a formula was found. Years later, to the apparent pleasure of listening auto workers, Lewis recounted the end of the strike. "And for long days and nights Mr. Knudsen said no, Donaldson Brown said no, and John Thomas Smith, the general counsel of the organization, said no. And we said yes, yes.

"And one morning, at three o'clock in the morning on one of the high floors of the Statler Hotel, Mr. Knudsen, the president, Donaldson Brown, chairman of the finance committee of the board, and John Thomas Smith walked into my room when I was in bed. And they had on their overcoats, and they had their hard hats in their hands, and their gloves on because the room was cold. I didn't get up, and they said that they would sign the contract at eleven o'clock that morning in Governor Murphy's office. And they did.

"So the impossible was accomplished."

The agreement signed that notable day recognized the United Auto Workers as the collective bargaining representative only of its members, a concession to the company's stubborn stand. In twenty plants, where

Lewis, Frank Murphy, and Walter Chrysler signing an agreement at settlement of the Chrysler strike in 1937. *Wayne State University Labor History Archives*

Union leaders leaving capitol building, Lansing, Michigan, at end of Chrysler strike. *Wayne State University Labor History Archives*

strikes had demonstrated the union's overwhelming strength, GM recognized the union as exclusive bargaining agent, not for union members alone, but for all employees. The company could not bargain with any other union without the Governor's consent—a massive breakthrough for the union. Collective bargaining on a national agreement was to begin four days later. Strikers were to be returned to their jobs without discrimination or penalty. These represented solid—and history-making —union gains.

The New York Times commented that Lewis had failed to establish his union as the "sole" bargaining agency. *Time* magazine said Lewis had been "badly beaten." William Green labeled it a "stinging defeat." Lewis pointed out, however, that seven weeks before, General Motors had said it had never dealt with a union and was not about to do so. Now, he noted, the company had signed a union contract. He added, with a touch of Lewis irony, "Part of the terms of settlement provide that members may wear their union insignia. Previously men had been discharged for doing so, and this made for confusion."

Looking back a few months later, the auto workers' convention declared, "The stay-in strike was beyond a doubt the only method by which the workers in the automobile industry could have forced the employers, who were determined to disregard the law of the land, into entering into real collective-bargaining relationships."

Edward Levinson, in his lively history of the CIO "march," observed, "The heads of the corporation were compelled, for the first time, to bargain with the spokesmen of their employees, the officers of the UAW and the CIO. . . . It broke the back of antiunionism in the most powerful industry in the world."

15 /

The Steel Workers Organize

"When is the trouble going to stop?"

From the very start, John L. Lewis had eyed the nation's great steel industry. Steel was a basic material, a vital ingredient in countless thousands of other industries. A tremor in steel would reverberate noisily in mills and factories in every corner of the land. "If we can organize here," Lewis said, "the rest will follow. . . . If the crouching lion can be routed, it is a safe bet that the hyenas in the adjacent bush may be scattered along the plain." Lewis knew, too, how heavily the fortunes of steel workers weighed on those of his miners. *Fortune* magazine commented, "As long as Big Steel is free to tack up a sign at a single pit head announcing a wage cut, the United Mine Workers are in danger of becoming, as they were once before, a mere 'rear guard' of labor's retreat to cooliedom."

Nor was the AFL blind to the significance of steel. In January, 1936, the Executive Council had turned down the organizing plan proposed by the Amalgamated Association of Iron, Steel and Tin Workers. The Association, traditional union of skilled steel workers, was a mere shadow, with fewer than 10,000 members and without a single national organizer in the mills. But the Council was not prepared to accept even this feeble brand of industrial unionism. Instead, it ordered Green to prepare a one-year plan for organizing steel workers in joint councils of craft unions. Lewis offered to raise 500,000 dollars for a joint campaign if the AFL would put up 1 million dollars. AFL leaders doubted that CIO unions could raise that much money.

Green called on affiliates to raise 750,000 dollars to finance a campaign in steel. He received pledges totaling 8,625 dollars. He offered the Association a joint campaign with other AFL "interested, affected and involved" unions. Lewis, on the other hand, offered to put up half a million dollars. He wanted mainly to be assured the union would retain its industrial scope.

The Association hesitated. When its officers asked for a meeting with Lewis, he answered sharply, "The policy of fluttering procrastination followed by your board is already responsible for the loss of some weeks of time and must be abandoned." The Board must make up its mind whether to "obstruct or cooperate. If you do not know your mind, please stay home." On June 4, 1936, the CIO announced the formation of the Steel Workers' Organizing Committee (SWOC).

The Committee took over from the Association the full power to bargain with employers and to set policy. (And the Association was scarcely heard of again.) Lewis appointed his longtime UMW associate, Vice President Philip Murray, as chairman. Murray moved fast. He set up offices throughout the steel country. Soon, SWOC organizers were sweeping into the steel towns. "Offices have been opened in towns that never before saw a union office," *Fortune* magazine reported. "Signs have been carried in streets where no union ever before dared to raise its head. And practically every day meetings are held in that vast territory, openly or furtively, in parks, in convention halls, in cockeyed shacks on the edges of town, or even on isolated farms leased for the occasion." SWOC staged a giant Fourth of July rally at Homestead, where the union had been driven out in the great strike of 1892. It met at Duquesne, too, whose mayor had vowed during the 1919 steel strike, "Jesus Christ himself" could not speak for the union in Duquesne.

Steel employers replied with a barrage of newspaper ads. Outsiders, the American Iron and Steel Institute charged, persons not connected with the industry, were running SWOC's campaign. They intended to use "coercion and intimidation . . . and foment strikes." Their goal was the "closed shop," the Institute charged, but the industry would fight any effort "to compel its employees to join a union or to pay tribute for the right to work." Collective bargaining, the ads contended, was already a fact in steel; the overwhelming majority of employees were represented in company-representation plans.

The companies increased their purchases of riot guns, tear-gas projectiles, tear-gas grenades, and gas masks. How could any man, Lewis wondered, go to church and worship God on Sunday, "knowing all the while that on Monday the company he represents will embark on a campaign of killing." He called the Institute's advertising campaign "a declaration of war" in an impending "battle for democracy." He accused the steel corporations of defying the Wagner Act, of "mulcting consumers, of co-ercing and spying upon its workers, and of foisting company unions upon them." The CIO's efforts, he promised, would be legal and peaceful.

SWOC's fast-moving organizers focused on the employee-representation plans—the company unions. They had been organized by the companies to offset independent, industry-wide unions. The SWOC encouraged the employee representatives to keep "biting at the heels of management." SWOC relentlessly exposed every mistake, every instance of arbitrary or dictatorial behavior by management. It claimed credit for even the slightest concession. When companies refused to give pay raises, SWOC pointed out that only an independent union could effectively insist. When U. S. Steel granted an increase, SWOC promptly claimed that it was done in fear of the union drive. *Barron's Weekly*, a prominent financial publication, commented: "For the first time . . . industrial management is faced with a labor movement which is smart and courageous, wealthy and successful. . . ." The company unions began to swing over to SWOC, sometimes intact, sometimes in bits and pieces. Before winter had passed, the SWOC claimed 200,000 members.

The drama of SWOC's drive was soon overshadowed by the tense battle in the auto plants. Some say Lewis planned it that way, pursuing a strategy of Napoleon's, "It is a good time to hit your adversary when he is looking in other fields." At that moment, another major figure was giving the matter serious thought. He was Myron C. Taylor, chairman of the board of U. S. Steel. He had spent the summer in Europe, punctuating his sightseeing with reflections on how to handle the threat of unionism. Whatever their philosophies, though, one January day found the two men dining at the same Washington hotel. Lewis and his luncheon partner, Senator Joseph Guffey of Pennsylvania, paused at the Taylor table and were presented to Mrs. Taylor. The Senator excused himself, but Lewis joined the Taylors and chatted for about twenty minutes. Mrs. Taylor, so *Fortune's* story goes, asked Lewis, "When is the trouble going to stop?"

"When your husband sits down and writes an agreement," Lewis replied.

"What are you doing tomorrow?" Taylor asked.

The two men met the next day in the first of a series of private discussions. The talks were interrupted when Lewis went to Detroit to take part in the General Motors negotiations and were promptly resumed when he returned.

On February 28, 1937, the two men reached agreement. Essentially they agreed that the steel workers had a right to choose their own bargaining representatives without interference and that U. S. Steel would sit down and negotiate with any such freely chosen representatives.

On March 2, in the offices of Carnegie-Illinois, largest of the U. S. Steel subsidiaries, the first contract was signed. Benjamin Fairless, sitting under a picture of Andrew Carnegie, the canny Scot who had founded the company, signed for the employer. In 1892, Carnegie's associate, Henry Clay Frick, had defeated the steel workers at Homestead in a bitter and violent dispute. Frick wired the vacationing Carnegie: "Do not think we will ever have serious labor trouble again. . . . We had to teach our employees a lesson and we have taught them one that they will never forget."

Carnegie cabled back: "Life worth living again. . . ."

Another Scot, Philip Murray, signed the historic document for the SWOC. "I wonder," he remarked, "what Carnegie would have thought of this."

It was a stunning achievement, a product of the times as well as of the two men who authored it. The Wagner Act had made collective bargaining national policy. The Walsh–Healey Act required corporations holding Government contracts to conform to Government standards— including, labor argued, the Wagner Act itself. Company unions seemed doomed, both by the Wagner Act and the SWOC drive. The La Follette Committee suspiciously eyed huge purchases of industrial munitions. Politically, the weight of the White House and of some state houses seemed likely to fall on the side of the union if trouble came. Both men were aware that the industry was making money for a change and that the British government was shopping for a steady, uninterrupted source of steel for its growing arms program. Lewis and the SWOC made effective use of the pressures generated by these favorable circumstances to achieve its historic breakthrough.

Lewis complimented Taylor, calling the settlement "a fine example of an intelligent approach to a great economic problem." Another steel-corporation president, Tom Girdler, said he was "shocked, even horrified by the news."

It sent great shock waves of hope through millions of

workers in the nation's mass-production industries. Together with the dramatic settlement of the General Motors sitdown, the U. S. Steel contract marked a major, historic achievement. Within a few weeks of each other, the two greatest bastions of the antiunion, open shop in the nation's industry had fallen.

A swollen torrent of steel workers poured into SWOC lodges. Companies by the scores signed up with the union. By the end of May, SWOC claimed 142 agreements and 375,000 members. But the union drive stalled when it met the companies that came to be known as "Little Steel": Republic, Inland, Bethlehem, and Youngstown Sheet and Tube. The firms met with SWOC representatives, but they refused to sign agreements. They built huge stores of weapons and gas and recruited private armies of armed guards and police. Little Steel's stand reflected, in part, the slacking-off of prosperity; business had slowed in the spring of 1937 and the economic future was clouded. It reflected, too, a pit-of-the-stomach antiunionism. Tom Girdler saw the union eating at the authority of management. "The boss is no longer the boss," he said.

SWOC called strikes on May 26, 1937, at twenty-seven plants belonging to Republic, Inland, and Youngstown. It extended the strike later to Bethlehem. Thousands of steel workers from Pennsylvania to Illinois answered the call. They were met promptly with violence and vigilantes. On the first day, a picket was killed at Canton, Ohio. His was the first of eighteen deaths during the strike, a prelude to a dispute seldom equalled in the nation's gloomy history of industrial violence and bitterness.

Four days later, on Memorial Day, strikers gathered in a vacant lot near the South Chicago plant of Republic Steel to protest police interference with their picket lines. The crowd listened quietly to the speeches, then moved in a loose, rambling body toward the plant to join the pickets. Near the plant, the police waited, drawn up in a loose line. Somewhere in the milling mass of strikers and sympathizers, someone tossed a tree branch—in the air or at the police, innocently or with malice, no one knows. A policeman fired and suddenly the crowd was engulfed in a drumfire of gunshots. It turned and ran, the police in hot pursuit. Ten marchers were killed: seven shot in the back, three in the side, none in front. Scores were injured, by clubs as well as guns.

The La Follette Committee's intensive investigation turned up no evidence that the strikers intended to storm the plant, as police claimed. Once violence had broken out, the Committee found, the strikers offered only token resistance. It characterized police conduct as "the most callous indifference to human life and suffering." Paramount Pictures refused to release its newsreel films of the episode; they were "not fit to be seen."

Lewis cried out, "Somewhere in this nation should be a force strong enough to bring these uniformed killers and their co-conspirators to justice. Somewhere in this nation should be a force greater than a steel company. Somewhere in this nation should be enough earnest and honest citizens to compel action by the Federal and state authorities. . . . Is labor to be protected or is it to be butchered?"

Armed deputies forced the way for food deliveries to

strikebreakers at a Youngstown Sheet and Tube plant. At Monroe, Michigan, two hundred special police opened the Republic plant. At Johnstown, Pennsylvania, a citizens' committee was formed to encourage strikers to return to work. Similar back-to-work efforts were launched, often with company sponsorship or company coordination, in other steel towns.

Efforts to mediate the strike failed. Faced with the inability of his mediation board to find a formula for settlement, irritated, perhaps, by a long season of strikes, President Roosevelt vented his feelings. "A plague o' both their houses," he exploded to reporters. The White House hastened to explain later that the President had meant only to condemn the "houses" of extremists on both sides—those who wanted violence, those who refused to negotiate. The CIO felt neither shoe fitted.

By mid-July the strike was defeated. Most plants were back in near-normal operation, many without any understanding with the union. The La Follette Committee summed up the strike. It was "no less brutal and violent" than other strikes in the industry had been. They were "more ominous," however, than the others because "the companies sought to incite a spirit of vigilantism in the citizens and and to subvert the community to strikebreaking activities." The companies were determined to flout the law and they tried, with a vigorous propaganda campaign, to enlist the help of local communities. Their activities were "dangerous to lawful government."

In time, the law of the land prevailed. That summer, the Supreme Court upheld the Wagner Act. Its ruling put the full force of Government behind the workers' right to organize and bargain collectively. In long, drawn-out proceedings before the National Labor Relations Board, Little Steel was eventually required to sign contracts with SWOC, pay millions in back wages, and restore jobs to hundreds of men they had fired because of union activities.

On Labor Day, Lewis voiced the agony of the steel workers. Eighteen steel workers, he reminded his listeners, "were either shot to death or had their brains clubbed out by police or armed thugs in the pay of the steel companies. The steel workers have now buried their dead, while the widows weep and watch their orphaned children become objects of public charity. The murder of these unarmed men has never been publicly rebuked by any authoritative officer of the state or Federal Government."

Labor's cause was just, he went on. "Its friends should not view its struggles with neutral detachment or intone constant criticism." He looked to the White House. "Labor, like Israel, has many sorrows. Its women weep for their fallen and they lament for the future of the children of the race. It ill behooves one who has supped at labor's table and who has been sheltered in labor's house to curse with equal fervor and fine impartiality both labor and its adversaries when they become locked in deadly embrace." And no one could doubt that he spoke directly to President Roosevelt.

Little Steel and the recession of 1937 slowed the powerful thrust of CIO's organizing drive. Its achievements, however, were beyond exaggeration. It had established industrial unions in the auto, steel, rubber, radio, and electrical-manufacturing industries. It had encouraged and sustained major organizing efforts in scores of other industries. It had recruited millions of workers into its unions. And it had spurred the AFL into its own intensive drive. Total union membership climbed from 3,738,000 in 1935, to 7,218,000 by 1937, to nearly 9 million by the end of the decade.

The recession underscored labor's most persistent problem. Steel mills slowed, then shut down. Assembly lines ground to a halt. Textile factories closed; tire factories slammed their gates. Thousands were put on part-time work; thousands more were thrown out of work. The CIO faced the problem, not of recruiting new members but of holding those it had.

Lewis insisted that every man, every woman, had a right to a job. "If the corporations which control American industry . . . fail to provide them with that job, then there must be some power somewhere in this land of ours that will go over and above and beyond those corporations with all their influence and power and provide a job and insure the right to live of that American. . . . If their union cannot help and protect them, their experience has been that no one else will." Labor must make sure that the responsibility for a job for every man "becomes the responsibility of the American people. . . ."

16 /
The March of the Unions

"Unity would have to wait"

Deep into the fall of 1936, Lewis toured the coal country, energetically urging the re-election of Franklin D. Roosevelt. From train platforms, union halls, and radio stations, he pounded away at the choice as he saw it, "between the malignant and selfish forces of reaction and the sorely beset forces of progress." He scoffed at Alfred M. Landon, the mild, onetime governor of Kansas, who was the Republican candidate. "Betimes," Lewis rumbled, "you have listened to the broadcasting of his diurnal and nocturnal babblements, as with quibble and quirk, he seeks to cozen the American people." He sang the praises of FDR: "The common people have proclaimed him a good and faithful servant and they stand as his protector."

Lewis had always been a Republican. He had supported Harding and Coolidge. He backed Hoover in 1928 and again in 1932 against the untested Roosevelt. The bitter trials of the twenties, the agonizing years of the depression, the upsurge of the New Deal, the burgeoning of the CIO—all these had tempered Lewis's hard-rock Republican loyalties. C. L. Sulzberger described him as "a mugwump pure and simple." Said Lewis, "I am not a Republican; I am not a Democrat; I am not a Fascist, a

Communist, nor a Socialist. I am for labor and I will go with anyone who will work for me in this cause." His cause, it became clear after 1933, was best served by Franklin Roosevelt, "a great liberal and humanitarian whose heart beats in sympathy with the heart beats of the common people."

When the Supreme Court killed the NRA and its protection for labor, some labor leaders moved to provide political support for labor's goals. Early in 1936, Lewis and Hillman joined forces to put the CIO hip-deep into the upcoming presidential campaign. They persuaded George L. Berry, head of the AFL Printing Pressmen, to join them. Berry had been associated with them in the NRA; he was politically active and politically ambitious. On April 2, they announced the formation of Labor's Non-Partisan League. Its immediate goal was to re-elect Roosevelt. In the long run, it hoped to provide "a rallying place for all liberal and progressive-minded voters of the nation."

From Big Rock, Virginia, a miner wrote to the *Journal:* "Under the Administration before President Roosevelt took his office we were loading coal by the acre, we were getting 60 cents for loading a five-ton car. Now a five-ton car brings us $2.35."

Lewis, too, reminded the miners of how they had prospered under Roosevelt. Not only that. "If I were consumed only by the desire to keep America out of European wars," Lewis told a Pottsville, Pennsylvania, rally, "I would vote for the re-election of President Roosevelt on this issue alone."

The League organized a quick and, in many areas, effective campaign. Labor's money, too, proved helpful. James McGregor Burns and Arthur M. Schlesinger, Jr., in their accounts of the campaign, repeat the story of Lewis's appearance at the White House, brandishing a 250,000-dollar check and accompanied by a photographer. FDR smiled, the report goes, but turned the check aside. "No, John, just keep it, and I'll call you if and when any small need arises." Lewis left, grumbling. In the end the story says, the Mine Workers' contributions came close to half a million dollars—"and without undue notice in the press." Secretary of Labor Perkins suggested that possibly, the President was not aware of the extent of Lewis's contributions. Lewis, on the other hand, insisted that the 500,000-dollar contribution was the figure named by the White House.

Labor's political effort, spearheaded by Lewis, the CIO, and the Non-Partisan League, contributed significantly to Roosevelt's unprecedented sweep. It provided the basis for Lewis's claim to White House help when the "economic royalists" sank "their fangs" into labor during the General Motors strike, and when Little Steel strikers were being battered by violence and propaganda. It contributed to the foundation on which the CIO built the historic auto and steel contracts and extended industrial unionism into the very heart of American industry. By mid-1937, when recession slowed the hectic pace, the CIO had carved out a significant place in the American scene.

Harold Laski, the brilliant British political scientist, met Lewis at a Washington dinner party. "For twenty years," he told Lewis, "I've been teaching my students that you represent the old, hopeless type of American labor leader, the corrupt racketeer who thinks only of his own power and lacks any progressive social vision. Now I have come back to America and my friends tell me that you are the new messiah. Was I wrong all these years? Or have you changed?" Lewis never replied.

At the end of 1937, a *Fortune* poll revealed that a sizable group of the American people, 38 percent, felt that unions needed reforming. Some of the hostility, *Fortune* concluded, reflected "a feeling that Lewis has overplayed his cards and brought a useful cause into disrepute."

Increasingly, Lewis was called on to define where he stood. "The aim of our movement," he told one interviewer, "is to organize the workers in order that they may obtain a larger participation in the benefits of modern industry. They have a legal right to organize. . . . We intend to enforce recognition of this right." He repeatedly singled out unemployment as the nation's major economic problem and returned to that theme time after time.

He never stood stronger in the United Mine Workers. He signed a new Appalachian agreement in 1937, raising the wages of northern workers to $6 a day, of southern workers to $5.60. It extended the seven-hour day to all mine workers.

Almost the only thorn in the union's side was Harlan County, Kentucky. The union had covered the area in 1933, but the contract had been allowed to lapse. When the union tried to return, a hotel where its organizers were staying was dynamited, a UMW car ambushed, and a volley of shots was fired into a UMW organizer's home, killing his small son. The La Follette Committee turned the spotlight of public hearings on the sorry state of affairs. The Government moved in with charges against forty-seven company officials and deputies of conspiring to deprive the miners of their legal rights. The jury deadlocked in the first trial. Rather than undergo a second trial, the operators signed a union contract.

Meanwhile, the split in the American trade-union movement was widened, then made permanent. The Tampa convention of the AFL in 1936 had confirmed the suspension of the CIO unions. In March, 1937, the CIO began forming state and local central bodies. Green complained that "the country seems to be filled with CIO organizers." He obtained a special anti-CIO tax of 1 cent per month per member to finance an aggressive organizing campaign. When the CIO held its first conference in October 1937, Phil Murray boasted that it is "now the dominant labor force in this nation." It seemed likely, though, that the AFL was close to its equal in numbers.

With some heavy-handed prodding from Lewis, the unity committees met again. For a moment, the possibility of reuniting the camps seemed bright, then abruptly faded. AFL partisans claimed that the committees had virtually reached an agreement. The CIO denied it; no basic industries had been marked for industrial unions, nor had the AFL unions waived claims to skilled craftsmen belonging to CIO unions.

Soon afterward, Lewis tossed out another peace proposal. He was prepared to recommend, he said, to the CIO's 4 million members that "they all walk into the American Federation of Labor, foot, horse, and dragoon the AFL to issue charters to all of these unions, and call a joint convention to work out the details." Or, the AFL could walk into the CIO on exactly the same terms.

In the spring of 1938, the heads of the thirty-eight CIO unions agreed to meet in convention in the fall to form a permanent national organization. Two years of fierce competition had only sharpened the differences between the two groups. The AFL's concern with jurisdiction meant little to most CIO unions. It meant little more to some AFL unions that were busily organizing on industrial lines, but the old slogans hung on. The AFL continued to resist government intervention in union affairs; the CIO saw it as useful, even necessary. The AFL unions, in the main, were headed by older men, veterans in their jobs. They were dubious about the younger men who had come to the fore in the newer CIO unions, who, in their turn, held no better opinion of them. And, too, Lewis was looking ahead—perhaps to greater place and power; perhaps to even more ambitious organizing projects. Unity would have to wait.

In November, the CIO met in Pittsburgh. Lewis reminded the delegates that, there, fifty-seven years before, almost to the day, Sam Gompers had founded the labor movement of his generation. "But time moves on and the old order changes," he said. "The labor movement and the type of organization founded in Pittsburgh fifty-seven years ago was not equal to the task of organizing or rendering service to the teeming millions who labor in American industries in this generation of our life." To take on this task, the Committee for Industrial Organization gave way to the Congress of Industrial Organizations. Its first president was John L. Lewis.

17

Lewis's Quarrel With FDR

"... a vote of no confidence"

Lewis had once urged Sam Gompers, just before World War I, to undertake a broad-scale organizing campaign. Gompers refused, explaining that it would disturb his friendship with President Wilson. Lewis vowed, then and there, he later recalled, that he would never allow himself or his union to become so deeply involved with a president or his administration that "in times of crisis the ties of loyalty and agreement and obligation . . . would paralyze me."

Lewis had asked help from Harding, Coolidge, and Hoover. He received little comfort and less aid. He found the Roosevelt Administration more friendly. He asked and often he received, though he came, in time, to believe that the price was too high.

In the dawn of the New Deal, Lewis remembered, FDR had opposed Section 7a. Lewis remembered, too how he had lobbied it through over the President's objections. "You see," he told Saul Alinsky, "I never trusted Roosevelt fully. Never." Still, in 1936, Lewis linked arms with the man he called "the greatest humanitarian of our times." Lewis said his eyes were wide open. "The

United Mine Workers and the CIO," he claimed afterward, "have paid cash on the barrel for every piece of legislation that we have gotten. . . . Is anybody fool enough to believe for one instant that we gave this money to Roosevelt because we were spellbound by his voice?"

The dust of the 1936 election had barely settled, though, when Lewis and the CIO joined battle with General Motors. It was then, Lewis told Alinsky some ten years later, "that I discovered the depths of deceit, the rank dishonesty and the double-crossing character of Franklin Delano Roosevelt." At the time, Roosevelt had been unwilling or unable to line up publicly with the sitdown strikers. His Administration, however, was pushing GM into negotiations with the CIO and toward a settlement. By a variety of devices, Lewis used his relationship with the White House to hint at even stronger pressures. It was not enough; Lewis appealed directly for help. FDR replied that "statements, conversations and headlines are not in order."

Lewis was even more deeply angered by the President's "plague o' both your houses" statement during the Little Steel strike that summer. The White House "clarification" didn't help, either, since it seemed to blame the violence on the CIO; the blame, in its eyes, clearly belonged on the steel companies. Lewis's coldly furious reply denounced the President for accepting labor's hospitality, then turning his back when "labor and its adversaries" became "locked in deadly embrace."

Angry as he was, Lewis was still not ready to force an open break. President Roosevelt's neutrality in labor disputes was still more useful than the antagonism of earlier administrations. Lewis was also looking ahead to plans which, without at least the Administration's silent consent, would be unworkable.

Increasingly, though, Roosevelt seemed to frustrate Lewis's plans and to blunt his ambitions. The recession that swept over the country in 1937–38 added fuel to their growing differences. "Americans cannot eat or live on platitudes or musical phrases," Lewis growled. "They want buying power." He warned the miners that they might have to fight wage cuts in 1938 as they had in the twenties. (He also told the miners that Roosevelt was "the only president in our lifetime who has tried to give a square deal to the common people of this country.") Soon, he was complaining to reporters that FDR was "getting nowhere fast," that he was "out-Hoovering Hoover." Lewis refused to take part in the President's birthday celebration, organized to raise money to combat poliomyelitis. He was busy, Lewis said, "working to get consideration and work relief and money for the millions now unemployed."

The rising clamor of industry leaders for curbs on the unions helped to maintain Lewis's shaky alliance with the Roosevelt Administration. The National Association of Manufacturers tried to kill the Wagner Act. Several states passed antiunion laws requiring union organizers to register, limiting picketing, prohibiting sitdown strikes, expanding the power of courts to issue injunctions against labor. Once more, in the 1938 Congressional elections, Lewis, the miners, and the CIO rallied behind FDR.

In 1939, Lewis again found himself at war with the

bituminous operators. The negotiations, he finally concluded, were "a ridiculous spectacle." When the contract expired on March 31, 1939, the miners stopped work. Lewis had offered to continue digging coal, but the operators had turned down all of his proposals. Lewis exploded in an angry letter: "Failure of the Roosevelt Administration to approve or sustain the mine workers' offer to keep the industry in operation caused many coal operators to believe that they had *carte blanche* from the Government to disembowel the mine workers' union if they could."

President Roosevelt told both parties bluntly that he wanted production resumed. "We might hold out against John L. Lewis," one operator said, "but we can't hold out against both Lewis and President Roosevelt."

In mid-August the world was stunned by the treaty between Nazi Germany and Communist Russia, until then avowed enemies. American Communists promptly switched party lines. They abandoned their "popular front" opposition to fascism and became strongly isolationist, opposing American defense preparations and entry or participation in foreign wars. The abrupt switch brought them into line with Lewis's increasingly vigorous stand against war and FDR's foreign policies. Then Germany invaded Poland, touching off the Second World War. A few days later, in a Labor Day speech, Lewis reminded the country again that the number of workers without jobs was not far less than it had been at the worst part of the depression. Even more strongly, he denounced the tone of President Roosevelt's foreign policy.

"Labor wants the right to work and live, not the privilege of dying . . . to sustain the mental errors of current statesmen." The CIO, too, opposed American involvement in the war. As a concession, though, to delegates supporting the Roosevelt foreign policy—Murray, Hillman, and others—the CIO added that it would "defend our country and our free institutions against foreign invasion."

Second only to the increasingly tense foreign policy debate, perhaps, was the question of a third term for Roosevelt. By the end of 1939, he had not said, possibly had not decided, whether he would defy the historic two-term tradition. The question came up one night in a meeting with Secretary of Labor Perkins and Teamster chief Dan Tobin. As Madame Perkins remembered it, the President mentioned a recent visit from John L. Lewis. Lewis had urged him to run for a third term, but the President had objected that he didn't think the people would like it. He had been thinking about that, Lewis replied. If the vice-presidential candidate happened to be John L. Lewis, most of the objections would disappear and FDR would be assured of both labor and liberal support.

Secretary Perkins noted her and Tobin's astonishment. "How did you answer him?" Tobin asked.

"He didn't press me," the President replied. "He just asked me to think it over and give it consideration."

James Wechsler told a similar story in his biography of Lewis. According to Wechsler, Lewis had suggested to FDR that the two of them would make an invincible ticket. The President considered the matter, then asked, "Which place will you take, John?"

Lewis flatly denied the story. He told Saul Alinsky that it had either been fabricated by the President himself— "a fantastic cock-and-bull tale he himself manufactured out of the whole cloth"—or was "typical Madame Perkins gossip."

In January, 1940, in an exultant mood, the miners' convention observed the United Mine Workers' golden anniversary. Virtually all of the nation's 600,000 coal miners carried UMW cards. The union held exclusive bargaining contracts throughout the bituminous- and anthracite-coal industries of the United States and Canada. The union treasury held some 2½ million dollars, enough, the officers reported, to withstand "any ordinary shock." Above all, the McDonald union history, published for the occasion, noted, "the coal miners are strongly cohesive and loyal to the principles of the union."

Lewis, though, had Roosevelt on his mind. The Roosevelt Administration, he told the delegates, had failed to solve the nation's problems of unemployment, low national income, mounting debt and taxes. Labor had lost touch with the Administration; it was without representation in the Cabinet or policy-making agencies of the Government and had no contact except an occasional interview with individual officials. The Democratic majority in Congress had baited and defamed labor without rebuke from Democratic leaders.

"I am one who believes," Lewis went on, "that President Roosevelt will not be a candidate for re-election." If the President insisted on running, Lewis predicted, and "dragooned" the Democratic convention into nominating him, he would reap only "ignominious defeat."

Some delegates defiantly said their local unions would support FDR. He "has done as much for us as any man in the United States today," said one. Another voiced the quandary of many, "In our local union there are two things that we all stand for. One is John L. Lewis; the other is Franklin Delano Roosevelt." The UMW convention, though, followed Lewis's lead. It shelved seventy-two resolutions urging a third term for Roosevelt and handed over the question of an endorsement to the Executive Board.

On May 28, President Roosevelt appointed Sidney

Meeting at State Fair Grounds, Detroit, 1940. (Left to right) Walter Reuther, Mayor E. Jeffries, Sidney Hillman, Philip Murray, Leo Krzycki, John L. Lewis. *Wayne State University Labor History Archives*

Hillman to the National Defense Advisory Commission. Lewis had not been consulted by either the President or Hillman. The appointment soon ballooned, in Lewis's mind, to a presidential raid on Lewis's chief lieutenants in the CIO, weaning away, he said, their "primary loyalty . . . from the CIO to himself."

As Hillman had taken his stand with FDR, so had other unions and union leaders. Lewis was the principal speaker at the convention of the Amalgamated Clothing Workers, but it endorsed a third term. David Dubinsky and the Ladies' Garment Workers joined the third-term supporters. Bill Green denounced Lewis as an "ingrate" for attacking the Administration. John Brophy returned from a Pennsylvania labor meeting with the conviction that the delegates, most of them miners, were supporting FDR.

"Don't they understand," Lewis growled, "that if Roosevelt is elected, it means war?"

The President called Lewis to the White House in an effort to square matters. The meeting ended, though, according to Saul Alinsky, in a bitter dispute.

The November 1 issue of the Mine Workers' *Journal* carried an article on page 1 speculating on which miner carried the oldest dinner pail in the coal-mining industry. "What a wonderfully interesting story these old dinner pails could tell." On page 2, under a quiet headline, the *Journal* noted briefly that John L. Lewis had endorsed Wendell L. Willkie for president. The Lewis speech on a nationwide radio network, in fact, had made front-page news all across the country. Again, Lewis had charged

Roosevelt with leading the nation into war and with failing to return labor's support. The "President has not sought nor seriously entertained" labor's views or advice. Roosevelt's election, Lewis declared, "would be a national evil of the first magnitude."

"It is obvious," Lewis went on, that President Roosevelt would not be re-elected without the overwhelming support of labor. "If he is, therefore, re-elected, it will mean that the members of the Congress of Industrial Organizations have rejected my advice and recommendations. I will accept the result as being the equivalent of a vote of no confidence, and will retire as president of the Congress of Industrial Organizations at its convention in November."

Lewis's startling endorsement of Willkie reunited him with his onetime antagonist, the Carpenters' Big Bill Hutcheson. But it separated him from many of his friends. The *Journal* reported after the election that it had received "numerous" letters from miners that were "severely critical" of Lewis's action. Lewis, the *Journal* explained, had merely expressed "his personal political views." It is doubtful, one historian noted, "whether Lewis had ever before espoused a policy so antithetical to the views of his rank and file."

Still, delegates to the CIO convention arrived at Atlantic City wearing "We want Lewis" buttons. Signs, placards, leaflets called on the convention to draft Lewis, rather than allow him to resign. When Lewis took the rostrum to open the convention, the delegates gave him a forty-three-minute ovation.

"I have done my work," he told them. "In just a day or two I will be out of this office."

Cries of "no, no," echoed from the floor. The draft-Lewis movement drew a part of its strength from the Communist and left-wing delegates who shared Lewis's isolationist views on foreign policy. It drew additional, if unmeasured, strength from some who were simply Lewis supporters.

Lewis was at his oratorical best in the days of discussion that followed. He opposed a resolution brought in by Hillman's followers urging AFL and CIO unity. His angry, derisive speech accused Dubinsky of abandoning his principles, derided Hillman and Zaritsky. He lampooned a proposal to "explore" the possibilities of unity. "Explore the mind of Bill Green? . . . I have done a lot of exploring in Bill's mind and I give you my word there is nothing there." Nor was there anything, he added, in "the mind of Bill Hutcheson . . . that would do you any good." He would waste no more time on it. "After all, I think there is a limit to which the membership of my organization should permit me to waste my time and their money."

Sidney Hillman had intended to stay at his desk in Washington on national-defense business. When he learned of the move to draft Lewis, however, he went to Atlantic City. When the session opened the next morning, Hillman was on the platform chatting amiably with friends. Soberly, he reminded the convention that French workingmen were in concentration camps. "Bombs are exploding in the workmen's sections in every part of

Britain. Labor in Britain is fighting. . . . Who wants to
live in a world dominated by scoundrels?"

Hillman praised Lewis. "I have considered my association with John L. Lewis the greatest privilege." But,
he went on, "I regret that John L. Lewis will not be the
leader of this organization. I know there is nothing that
he can do and will do and will agree to do but what he
believes to be the best for the organized-labor movement."

"Coldly, logically," Hillman killed the draft-Lewis
movement, Labor Reporter Louis Stark wrote the next
morning in *The New York Times*. Lewis himself nominated Philip Murray to succeed him as president of the
CIO.

Taking leave of the delegates, Lewis dramatically con-
trasted the plight of 52 million people "who do not have
enough to eat" and of the 23 million farmers "who cannot sell their foodstuffs at prices that will give them a
return.

"And then in the face of that condition some of us become so confused that we do not hold to accountability
those of our statesmen who in long years have done
nothing for that fifty-two million and make no promises
to do anything for them in the future. Well, what are you
going to do about it? You are well fed. So am I. You are
not hungry. Neither am I. What are we going to do?"

As for his leaving, "We cannot stop to weep and wear
sackcloth and ashes because something that happened
yesterday did not meet with our approval, or that we
did not have a dream come true. . . . You know when you

first hired me I was something of a man and when I leave
you in a day or two I will still in my own mind be something of a man. . . ." Many delegates, Alinsky observed,
"felt they were hearing a man preach his own funeral
eulogy."

To the miners' convention two years later, Lewis explained that he had retired voluntarily. "Those of you
who were there know that that convention would have
re-elected me unanimously had I chosen to run. I was
glad to get out." The miners had paid the bills, and its
leaders had showed the way, for the CIO and for "a modern labor movement in this country." Now, he added, he
had, in his "mind's eye" plans that would put "more
bread and butter on the kitchen table of every coal miner
in America. . . ."

Alinsky later suggested to Lewis that his bet on Willkie
was "a wild gamble that was politically pointless." It was
no gamble, Lewis replied; he had had no doubt that
Roosevelt would be elected. But he had to get out of the
CIO if he were to achieve unity in the labor movement.
Alinsky doubted that labor unity at the time had been
anywhere "in the vicinity of Lewis's mind."

18

Preparations for World War II

"The rift within the lute"

When the miners went on strike in April, 1941, Lewis explained why. Without a contract, he said, "our men would be arrested for trespassing and you know I would never want to see this happen." Harry S. Truman, the senator from Missouri and chairman of the Senate committee investigating the national-defense program, wanted to know more.

Seventy percent of the coal operators in this country and the United Mine Workers are in agreement, Lewis told the committee. Thirty percent are in disagreement. "The rift within the lute," he said, was the refusal of southern operators to give up the wage differential that had kept their wages lower than those in the northern mines. "The tail of the industry is undertaking to vigorously wag the dog." The union is "afraid," he went on, of "the arrogant, insolent, economic, political and financial power" of the southern operators.

Shouldn't wages be the same? Truman asked. "Don't they produce just as much coal per man?"

Lewis agreed. "A track layer in the South anywhere lays just as much track as a track layer in Pennsylvania

or Ohio. A timber man sets just as much timber. . . .
There is no difference in the efficiency of labor. The difference is a pound of bacon a day per man to those day
men—it just amounts to a pound of bacon a day. . . ."

"We in Missouri would like to sell it to them," Truman
interposed.

"I understand you have some hog meat for sale down
there," Lewis responded, "and if we get this forty cents
I will agree that we will eat some of your hog meat."

In the end, the North-South differential was elimi-
nated, setting what the *Journal* proclaimed "the highest
hourly rates in the history of the bituminous coal industry"—1 dollar an hour, 7 dollars for a seven-hour day.
The miners also got their first paid vacations and a voice
in administering the medical services that were bought
with checkoffs from their pay. "Tin money"—that notori-
ous scrip that could be used only at the company store—
was prohibited.

Even as the miners went back to the pits, the war
swelled with growing violence. In the summer of 1941,
Germany turned on the Soviet Union, its recently ac-
quired ally. Now the conflict tortured nearly half the
globe, and Americans were uneasy under its gloomy
shadow. Many were sure that war was near despite vast
ocean barriers; others failed or refused to see. The Roosevelt Administration moved more energetically to build
the nation's defenses and strengthen its armed forces.

Lewis opposed any American participation in the
world conflict. Even so, he battened down the hatches in
preparation for the storm that he seemed sure was ahead.

He settled the anthracite and bituminous contracts, then turned to a piece of long-standing unfinished business.

Earlier that year, the H. C. Frick Coal Company, a subsidiary of U. S. Steel, had finally disbanded the last of the company unions at its mines. Fayette county—all of it, after close to twenty years—was unionized. "The best news I've heard in a long, long time," a miner said. "I learned a lesson under nonunion conditions that if I live for two thousand years I shall never forget." Now Lewis demanded the same union shop in the captive mines that prevailed in the rest of the industry. Once a man had a job and shared the benefits of the union's bargaining, he was required, under a union shop, to join the union to keep his job. The operators balked and Lewis called out the men—some 53,000 of them.

They returned within the week under a temporary truce, while the National Defense Mediation Board considered the question. Finally it refused to act on it. The miners prepared to stop work again. President Roosevelt asked Lewis to delay the walkout, but Lewis refused. The next day, President Roosevelt again stressed the urgent need for uninterrupted production of coal.

Lewis's reply was haughty. "If you would use the power of the State to restrain me, as an agent of labor," he wrote, "then, Sir, I submit that you should use that same power to restrain my adversary in this issue, who is an agent of capital. My adversary is a rich man named Morgan, who lives in New York. . . ."

Lewis denied that the dispute impaired defense output; it's only a fight between a labor union and a ruthless corporation. Lewis offered to meet with the President and with "my adversary, Mr. J. P. Morgan, for a forthright discussion of the equities of this problem."

That day, the miners quit work again.

President Roosevelt replied curtly that whatever Lewis's dispute with Morgan, the question of an adequate fuel supply was "of greater interest and import to the national welfare. There is every reason for the continuance of negotiations. There is no reason for stoppage of work." For the third time, the President asked Lewis and the miners to resume digging coal. Lewis ignored the appeal, as he had those before it.

An irritated Congress was barely restrained by other labor people and by the Administration from clamping tough legal curbs on the entire labor movement. The President, angry and frustrated, snapped that defense production would not be "hampered by the selfish obstruction of a small but dangerous minority of leaders for a minute."

At that moment, an observer said, Lewis was "the most cordially hated man in America."

Once again the miners went back to work, and the dispute was sent back to the National Defense Mediation Board. On November 10, 1941, the Board denied the union shop by a vote of 9 to 2; even the AFL representatives voted against the miners. Philip Murray and Thomas H. Kennedy, both miners, cast the two dissenting votes, then, the next day, angrily resigned. Other CIO representatives gave up their places on Mediation Board panels. Their protests and resignations ended the Board's usefulness.

The miners prepared to renew their strike. Roosevelt warned the miners that the government would not order what he incorrectly labeled a "closed shop." It would never compel the small (five percent) minority of non-members to join the union. The miners walked out for the third time on November 19.

The President asked the union and the industry to put aside the dispute while the war lasted or to let an impartial umpire decide it. Lewis balked; it was doubtful, he insisted, that an unprejudiced umpire could be found. The President went ahead, anyway. He appointed a three-man board to settle the question. It consisted of Lewis, Benjamin Fairless, president of U. S. Steel, and Dr. John R. Steelman, director of the U. S. Conciliation Service. Steelman had been instrumental in settling the miners' contract disputes in 1939 and earlier in 1941. Lewis promptly accepted. Many, probably Lewis himself, saw the board as a roundabout way of handing the captive miners their union shop.

Fairless argued, "John, it's just as wrong to make a man join the union if he doesn't want it as it is to dictate what church he should belong to."

Lewis countered, "It's wrong to have men getting the benefit of better hours and conditions won for them by the union without giving a penny to help support the union." Steelman voted, as expected, for the union shop. The decision was announced Sunday morning, December 7, 1941.

During the uneasy Nazi–Soviet truce, the Communist left had supported Lewis in his opposition to Roosevelt's foreign policy. It deserted him when the Nazi panzers turned on the Soviet Union in the summer of 1941; now it backed FDR's call to make America "the arsenal of democracy," supplying arms to its allies. Lewis turned to his long-time associate, Phil Murray, pleading with him to join in opposing Roosevelt's foreign policies. During a long, emotional walk along the Atlantic City boardwalk, the two old partners argued. Finally Lewis said, "Well, from now on, Philip, you go your way and I will go mine." Murray protested, but Lewis turned away. "It was nice to have known you, Phil."

Later, Murray charged that Lewis had been "hell bent on creating national confusion and national disunity." When war came, Lewis gave his support in his own fashion.

In January, 1942, Lewis surprised both Phil Murray and William Green with a new proposal to renew labor-unity negotiations. ". . . If accouplement could be achieved," he wrote, "with unified and competent leadership, the results would be advantageous and in the public interest."

The New York Times reported that Lewis and some AFL leaders had already agreed on the new leadership. Despite the reports, Green said the AFL was ready to meet, but Murray exploded angrily. "I will not be Pearl Harbored," he said. He reminded Lewis that any unity talks would have to be arranged through the office of the president of the CIO. Lewis retorted that he, Lewis, was chairman of a CIO Unity Committee appointed in 1939 and never discharged. As such, he claimed ample authority to participate in negotiations.

President Roosevelt stepped in, in the interest of national unity or perhaps to spike his old antagonist's guns. He invited AFL and CIO representatives to join in a joint Victory Board. It would insure maximum labor participation in the war program and focus attention on winning the war. Lewis's proposed "accouplement" was soon forgotten.

Lewis did not forget, though. Soon afterwards, he handed the CIO a bill for 1,665,000 dollars, representing only a small part of the 7,249,304 dollars the miners had invested in building the CIO. "Don't think I don't know," Lewis told the miners, "what it means to load coal in bad air, under bad trap, in water, amid hazards of explosions and dust" to raise that money. The UMW said it was merely asking the CIO to credit two months' per capita tax against the outstanding loans. But the CIO refused to recognize the loans. The Mine Workers refused to pay any more dues. So ended the history-making alliance of the miners and the CIO.

That summer the Steel Workers Organizing Committee converted itself into the United Steelworkers of America and made Murray its first president. The miners' Policy Committee accused Murray of making "false, malicious and defamatory" statements about Lewis and the UMW. Murray had broken faith with the miners, the Committee charged, and cast his lot "with the Communistic element of the CIO"—Lewis's former supporters. After a lengthy trial by his UMW associates and days of bitter argument, Lewis abruptly cut off the proceedings. He simply removed Murray—"My former friend," he described him—

as vice president of the Mine Workers, because Murray was now a full-time official of another union.

"There is an ancient maxim, it's just as ancient as civilization," Lewis told the Policy Committee, "'whose bread I eat, whose song I sing.' And I am saying to you that the men who eat the Mine Workers' bread in this country should sing the Mine Workers' song. There is nothing obtuse or mathematical or fourth dimensional about that statement, because everyone understands it, it is one of the basic elements of life. My father taught it to me, as your fathers taught it to you."

That fall, on September 9, 1942, Myrta Bell Lewis, the gentle-spoken country schoolteacher who had stood quietly by the side of this tempestuous man for thirty-five years, died.

19

Lewis Fights His War

"... the greatest united showing
of hands in history"

"The coal miners of America are hungry.

"They are ill-fed and undernourished below the standard of their neighbors. . . . When the mine workers' children cry for bread, they cannot be satisfied with the 'Little Steel formula.' When illness strikes the mine workers' families, they cannot be cured with an anti-inflation dissertation."

In this dramatic vein, Lewis opened contract negotiations in March, 1943. Industry was guaranteed its costs and a profit to boot, no matter how much prices rose, Lewis declared. But the nation's workers were held to a maximum increase of 15 percent, the War Labor Board's (WLB) estimate of how much living costs had risen since January 1, 1941—the so-called Little Steel Formula. But price controls had never really reached the remote towns where coal was mined, Lewis argued. Thousands of miners had walked out in wildcat strikes earlier that year, but Lewis counseled them to go back to work and wait for the time, just ahead, when they would no longer be bound by a contract.

The nation would need about 700 million tons of coal

in this wartime year, Lewis reminded the operators. The miners would need "strong meat" to do the job. They wanted a 2 dollars a day raise. They wanted the operators to pay for safety devices, blacksmithing of tools, and the "bug lights" they wore on their hard hats. They wanted portal-to-portal pay, too. Often miners traveled as long as an hour and a half from the mine portal to the work face, then back at the end of the shift. They were paid, though, only for the time they actually worked at the face. Travel pay was common practice in hard-rock mines and in coal mines of other countries, the miners contended; now they, too, wanted to be paid for it.

As the end of the contract neared, President Roosevelt urged the union and operators to keep on negotiating without stopping work. With somewhat the same purpose in mind, Senator Truman again invited Lewis to appear before his Senate investigating committee. Lewis replied that he would come if negotiations permitted it. The committee counsel, however, "commanded" him to appear. Lewis called the counsel's letter "contemptuous." The counsel replied with a subpoena legally ordering Lewis to appear.

An angry Lewis took the witness stand. The Government itself was creating inflation by giving industry "excessive rewards," Lewis said, but denying the worker equal consideration. Wage increases were limited by Government formula; the worker had no way of keeping up with rising living costs; he was considered unpatriotic if he asked for improvement.

Industry was allowed to put aside money to replace its

plant and machines, Lewis argued. The worker, however, would come out of the war older in years, weaker in body, his assets eaten up, his maintenance long deferred. But corporations would not have to make these sacrifices. Congress could not condone a policy, he contended, that fattened industry and starved labor.

Senator Ball interrupted. "Surely you are not contending that any worker is not getting enough to eat? If so, that is demagoguery pure and simple and you know it is."

Lewis flushed angrily. "When you call me a demagogue before I can reply, I hurl it back in your face, sir. And I say, sir, when you call me a demagogue, you're less than a proper representative of the people of this country."

Senator Truman rushed in to quell the outburst. "We don't stand for any sassy remarks," he told Lewis. "I don't like that remark to a member of this committee."

Lewis said innocently, "Who cast the first stone?"

Lewis explained. The miners were not getting enough to eat "in the sense that it maintains their strength. The coal mine burns a man out pretty fast." He noted that a miner worked for 1 dollar an hour, a carpenter in New York for $1.80. It was not just.

Lewis pointed out that the coal industry had obtained a price increase of 22 cents a ton to pay overtime for work on the sixth day each week. But more than half of the industry was still working only five days. It simply pocketed the extra 22 cents a ton. "Their profit is greater by not working on Saturdays," Lewis said.

"We want help," Senator Burton then commented, "to

make sure we don't start off inflation from this corner."

"Do you mind," Lewis persisted, "first inflating the stomachs of my members?"

Early in April, with an eye cocked at the restless miners, President Roosevelt called on the nation "to hold the line" against further increases in prices or wages. An attempt, Lewis complained, "to make the rich man more affluent and the poor more despairing."

City workers might get by on two and a half pounds of meat a week, miners' wives complained, but how could a miner's family live on it? One miner's wife said simply, "My children are half-dressed and they don't get the right things to eat. Prices of food are so high that we can't afford to buy what we need and half the time my husband goes to work with only bread and butter in his bucket."

The operators were not really negotiating. They were relying on the Little Steel Formula and the President's "hold-the-line" order to limit any pay increase the miners might get. They were quite willing to let the War Labor Board decide how little it would be.

Eight days before the strike deadline, the Board began hearings on the coal dispute. Almost as promptly, the miners began leaving the pits. On May 1, 1943, they all stayed home.

President Roosevelt ordered Secretary of the Interior Harold Ickes to seize the mines and operate them in the name of the United States Government. That Sunday morning Lewis and the miners' committee met with Ickes in Washington. At almost that moment, too, the

President was preparing to broadcast an appeal to the miners to return to work. The miners agreed to a truce and returned to New York to get Policy-Committee approval. Shortly after nine o'clock, Lewis phoned Ickes that the Committee had agreed to return to the mines. At nine forty-four, the *Journal* noted, Lewis told reporters that he had ordered the miners to reopen the mines on Tuesday, May 4. At ten o'clock, the President went on the air. He made no reference to the miners' decision to end the strike; instead, "not as President, not as Commander-in-chief, but as the friend of the men who work in the mines," he asked the miners to resume digging coal the next day, Monday.

The men went back to work—most of them, though, on Tuesday, as Lewis had asked. Secretary Perkins remembered the President's comment, "I have learned one thing. The mine workers won't vote for President of the United States as John L. Lewis tells them, but they won't do what I tell them on matters that have to do with their union activities."

The War Labor Board resumed hearings on the dispute, though the union ignored the proceedings. A growing barrage of anger and abuse was leveled at Lewis. His actions triggered renewed attacks on unions generally. In Congress, numerous bills threatened to restrict and circumscribe labor's right to strike and bargain collectively.

On May 21, the War Labor Board denied the miners' bid for a wage increase. It suggested further negotiations on portal-to-portal pay, but it improved the miner's vacation pay and required operators to pay for safety devices, blacksmithing, and headlamps. Labor members thought the miners were entitled to a raise. "Failure of price regulation," they said, "makes imperative that wage regulation must be realistically adjusted."

On June 1, 1943, the miners again stayed home.

President Roosevelt angrily ordered the miners back to work. "I must remind the miners that they are working for the Government on essential war work and it is their duty no less than that of their sons and brothers in the armed forces to fulfill their war duties." He told Ickes to reopen the mines. Ickes laid down the law to Lewis; he expected Lewis to direct the members of the United Mine Workers to return to work.

"I have no power to direct," Lewis replied softly. "I shall, however, recommend to the Policy Committee of the United Mine Workers of America that it direct the mine workers to return to work."

The mines reopened June 7, but this did little to soften the abuse heaped on Lewis and the miners. Southern Democrats and conservative Republicans, anxious to cut back labor's growing strength, denounced them. Editorial writers, commentators, and columnists unleashed their sharpest epithets. An Army newspaper declared that Lewis's activities "have entered the realm of treason." Many sections of labor worried that Lewis's stand would bring down the wrath of Congress on the entire labor movement.

On June 12, the Senate passed the Smith–Connally Act and sent it to the White House. The bill reaffirmed the

President's power to seize an industry threatened by a work stoppage. Anyone interfering with an industry under Government seizure in any way—by strike, lockout, or slowdown—could be fined 5,000 dollars or sent to prison. The bill was clearly aimed at Lewis.

On June 18, the War Labor Board stamped approval on its panel's findings. It added a requirement of a new, two-year contract firmly prohibiting strikes for the duration of the war. A "yellow-dog contract," Lewis called it. It "would place political and economic manacles and leg irons on each of the members of the union." The combination of the Board's antagonistic ruling and the threat of the Smith–Connally Act produced the inevitable result. The miners quit work for the third time. Ickes and Lewis quickly arranged a four-month truce, but Lewis insisted that if the mines were returned to private operation before October 31, the truce would automatically end.

The anger directed at Lewis and the miners, though, refused to die. On June 25, in less than two hours, Congress passed the Smith–Connally Act over President Roosevelt's vigorous veto. Some Congressional leaders hailed it as "a body blow to Lewis."

Soon afterwards, though, Lewis announced that he had reached an agreement with the Illinois operators. The WLB, however, refused to approve it. It was not a "genuine settlement," it said, since it covered outside men (who were not affected by underground travel) as well as underground workers. The miners and the Illinois operators produced a second agreement, and the WLB cut 37½ cents from the $1.50 raise that Lewis had negotiated. He angrily labeled the WLB action a pay cut. Once again, work stoppages began breaking out. On November 1, 1943 over half a million miners, bituminous and anthracite, "took a holiday," as the *Journal* put it, "of their own accord, without a single work stoppage order. . . . It was the greatest united showing of hands in the history of the American labor movement."

Once more, Ickes took over the mines. He and Lewis juggled travel time and lunch time and overtime and came out with an $8.50 a day wage. The miner got his $1.50 raise, but he also worked longer hours. Once again, the miners went back to the mines. When the WLB finally finished tinkering with the agreement, the miner's weekly wages came to $57.07 for a 48-hour week. Under the old contract, it had been $45.50 for a 42-hour week. It just about matched Lewis's starting bid of a 2 dollars a day raise.

A few months later, Lewis spoke up in a *Collier's* article. "Political malignity, springing from a determination to destroy all who cannot be controlled, has conducted an organized campaign against us," he charged. Trivial strikes had disrupted the nation's war effort, but neither leaders nor strikers had been named and pilloried. "No clarion from the White House starts the hue and cry against them."

In 1944, an incensed and defiant Lewis opened the miners' convention. The miners, he trumpeted, seek equality in the nation's economic life, recognition of their rights to a point where "they are privileged to live like men, lending a helping hand to all unfortunates." But what did they get? Miners were setting production records and "dying at a faster rate in the coal mines than is the case on some battlefields." Lewis hurled his angry defiiance at "the smug faces of some of those who denounce the Mine Workers, whether he be a coal operator, a manufacturer, a Russian pants maker, or the President of the United States—what difference does it make?

"Well, we finally got something, after the President had publicly kicked every coal miner in this country in the face . . . denouncing [this union's] officers and asking us to call off the strike, when we had agreed that afternoon to his representatives that we would call off the strike. . . . How do you like it? Perhaps you would like a little more of it?

"Well, vote him into office in November, and I think you will have some more of it next April."

20 /
The Miners' Postwar Battles

"We accuse. . . ."

Under Lewis's guiding hand, the Mine Workers' convention in 1944 formally regretted that it had endorsed Roosevelt in 1936. It would not make the same mistake again. Roosevelt had "abolished" collective bargaining, the convention declared, substituting dictatorial orders of Government agencies. His veto of the Smith–Connally Act was "left-handed." He had opposed the union in the captive-mine strike and in the 1943 bituminous strike. His appeal to striking miners, even though he knew the Policy Committee had already agreed to return to work, was not only unfair but "an outrageous exhibition of personal malice."

The miners endorsed Governor Thomas E. Dewey of New York—a believer in equal justice, the convention said, fearless and courageous. The Republican platform, too, promised "recognition and representation" for labor.

Ironically, two years before, Dewey had described Lewis as "a frustrated man whose every previous effort to fasten himself and his views on the American people has been repudiated."

Roosevelt, for his part, had singled out Lewis as "that

one labor leader who had blemished labor's wartime achievements." Roosevelt, of course, won easily.

Days past the April 1 contract deadline, with miners leaving the pits in growing numbers, Lewis announced an increase in the miners' pay and vacation bonus. But the announcement was buried under the news that same day (April 12, 1945) that Franklin Delano Roosevelt had died at Warm Springs, Georgia. The *Journal* expressed its "shock" and wished Vice President Harry S. Truman success.

Lewis opened 1946 negotiations in a grim mood. He hoped that the union and operators could negotiate a new peacetime contract. Miners were bringing out 2 million tons of coal every working day—4,000 tons every productive minute. But they had increased their earnings only by working longer hours. And even worse, to achieve that unprecedented record, Lewis continued, "we killed in the coal mines outright an average of one thousand, nine hundred and eighty-one men a year. We crushed and injured in a year an average of sixty-six thousand, nine hundred and sixty-eight."

"By the record," he charged, the operators, "through mismanagement, cupidity, stupidity and wanton neglect made dead twenty-eight thousand mine workers . . . violently mangled, crushed and shattered the bodies of one million, four hundred thousand mine workers. . . .

"We accuse, by the record, that the industry extorts annually from the pay envelope of the mine workers sixty millions of dollars for pseudo, hypothetical and substandard medical services, hospitalization and insurance of an

Miners waiting for the man-trip to take them into the mine.
Bureau of Mines, U.S. Department of the Interior

actual value of less than one-third of the aforesaid sixty million dollars. . . .

"We demand abatement of this slaughter.

"We demand cessation of the accompanying extortion."

These were the union's only "demands" on the operators. Lewis's accusation was an act, an employer spokesman told reporters. "The Mine Workers ask for bread," Lewis replied, "and they are given a stone."

The bituminous contract would expire March 31, Lewis ominously reminded the union's officers and members. "No agreement will be in existence after the above-given date. Until present negotiations are completed, each member will be governed accordingly." On April 1, 1946, the miners stopped work.

Negotiations dragged on day after day. Finally, after a long brooding silence, Lewis read the operators a statement, "For four weeks we have sat with you; we attended when you fixed the hour . . . departed when weariness affected your pleasure. . . .

"When we sought surcease from bloodletting, you professed indifference. When we cried aloud for the safety of our members, you answered, 'Be content—'twas always thus.'

"When we urged that you abate a stench, you averred that your nostrils were not offended.

"When we emphasized the importance of life, you pleaded the priority of profits. . . .

"You profess annoyance at our temerity; we condemn your imbecility.

"You are smug in your complacency; we are abashed by your shamelessness; you prate of your respectability; we are shocked at your lack of public morality. . . .

"To cavil further is futile. We trust that time, as it shrinks your purse, may modify your niggardly and antisocial propensities.

"Good day, gentlemen. It's been nice knowing you."

With that, he walked out.

As May came on, President Truman summoned Lewis to the White House. Three hours before he was due there, Lewis announced that the miners would go back to the pits for two weeks as their "contribution to the nation's economy." The operators offered to settle for an increase of 18½ cents an hour. That had been the settlement in the lengthy strike at General Motors, at General Electric, and in the steel industry. But Lewis had something else in mind.

He wanted a welfare fund. He had said so from the start. He proposed the operators pay into the fund a specified sum of money for each ton of coal the miners dug. The fund would provide:

1. Adequate and modern medical services. "We plan to replace the present company-doctor scourge."

2. Adequate hospitalization under proper standards.

3. Life insurance. The miner paid nearly three times as much as a sedentary worker.

4. Rehabilitation. Probably some 50,000 miners incapacitated by on-the-job accidents had been abandoned without assistance or training.

5. Economic aid in distress or hardship cases. Company doctors, Lewis charged, frequently manipulated workmen's compensation cases to deny the injured worker all or part of the benefits due him.

If any money were left, Lewis concluded, it would be used for "cultural and educational work."

The welfare fund quickly became the core issue. Lewis insisted that it would cost the operators nothing, for it would come out of the money the public paid for coal. Operators complained that it taxed them for "social welfare." They proposed, instead, a fund made up of contributions from both operators and miners and administered in hardship cases by the Red Cross.

The Bituminous Coal Institute announced it would ask Congress to outlaw any royalty payments on coal for a health and welfare fund. Lewis declared flatly that "the Mine Workers have no intentions to negotiate a contract now or later that does not provide for such a fund and for such protection to the mine worker."

On May 21, the miners were due to walk out again at the very moment the railroad unions were preparing to strike. President Truman ordered Secretary of the Interior A. J. Krug to take over operation of the mines, then personally went before Congress to ask for a tough law punishing union leaders who called a strike and workers who went on strike against the Government. The recalcitrant railroad unions yielded; Lewis and Krug went into intense negotiations in the coal dispute.

A week later, they emerged with an agreement. It represented, the *Journal* proclaimed, "the greatest economic and social gains registered by the United Mine Workers of America in a single wage agreement since the birth of the union in 1890." It provided:

1. An 18½ cent an hour wage increase.

2. A welfare and retirement fund, financed by a royalty of 5 cents a ton; present deductions from miners' pay for medical care would be put into a medical and hospitalization fund.

3. A comprehensive survey by the Coal Mines Administration of hospital and medical facilities, housing, sanitation, and other living conditions in the coal regions.

4. Increased vacation pay of 100 dollars.

5. A new safety code to be issued by the Federal Bureau of Mines, recognizing local mine-safety committees set up by local unions to report dangerous conditions.

The agreement marked both a leap forward and a significant change in direction. Operators had once completely controlled medical and hospital expenditures, though miners had paid for them by deductions from their pay. Now these expenditures were greatly expanded; employers were required to contribute to the cost; and they were placed under joint labor-management direction. The Bureau of Mines was given greater powers to deal with unsafe conditions in the mines. The miners were given an even-more-important voice in maintaining a safe work place. But few—not miners, operators, or government, probably not even Lewis himself —foresaw the near-revolutionary impact of the newly born welfare fund. It would add, in the years just ahead, an almost totally new dimension, health care, to collective bargaining and union contracts throughout the nation's economy.

That first postwar year, 1946, was turbulent. A record 4,600,000 workers—more than 7 percent of the nation's work force—stopped work, giving up 116 million mandays of work. Strikes erupted at General Motors, in the soft-coal industry, on the railroads, and in thousands of other industries and firms. Industrialists, congressmen, editorial writers, and commentators aimed accusing fingers and angry words at the unions. Congress turned down President Truman's angry proposal to draft strikers into the armed forces. Instead, it passed the almost equally vindictive and punitive Case Bill. President Truman vetoed it, arguing it would not stop strikes. The House upheld his veto by the skimpy margin of five votes. Soon, though, Congress would vent its anger in the Taft–Hartley Act.

There was an uneasy peace in the coal fields, too. The operators objected to many provisions of the Krug–Lewis agreement. The union objected to the way the Coal Mines Administration was interpreting it. Secretary Krug at first refused, then reluctantly authorized negotiations on the miners' complaints. He finally told Lewis that the union's proposals were of "such a fundamental nature" that they should be taken up with the operators. After all, the Government was only the interim custodian. Lewis refused. The union's contract was with the Government, he said. Then Lewis announced the union would terminate the contract on November 20, 1946.

Krug promptly denied the union had any such right. President Truman promised an "uncompromising fight" to back Krug's stand.

Two days before Lewis could act, though, Federal Judge Alan T. Goldsborough prohibited him and the Mine Workers from terminating the Krug–Lewis contract. By nightfall, miners began leaving their jobs; the strike was virtually in full force by the following day. Cities dimmed their lights to conserve coal. Railroads reduced passenger services. Federal buildings were ordered to reduce their temperatures to 68 degrees. Some gloomy observers predicted that a prolonged coal strike would throw 25 million workers out of work.

Lewis and the Mine Workers were charged with contempt of court, and Judge Goldsborough found them guilty. The strike, he commented, "is an evil, demoniac, monstrous thing that means hunger and cold and unemployment and destitution and disorganization of the social fabric; a threat to democratic government itself."

Lewis labeled the ruling an "ugly recrudescence of 'government by injunction.'"

The judge fined the union 3,500,000 dollars, Lewis himself, 10,000 dollars. Just as President Truman was about to go on radio to discuss the strike, Lewis announced the miners would return to work. In due course, the Supreme Court upheld the Goldsborough ruling, though it reduced the fine on the union to 700,000 dollars provided that it reinstated the Krug–Lewis agreement. Lewis and the union complied.

At almost that moment an explosion at the Centralia Coal Company Mine Number 5 in Illinois killed 111 of the 142 workers in the mine. An official union circular hotly charged: "Criminal negligence on the part of [Secretary] Krug is responsible for the death of these brave men and the future impoverishment of their families. Forced to work by yellow-dog injunction secured by Krug and his co-conspirators, the safety of these men was neglected to a point where they died like trapped animals. . . . This killing must stop. . . . Coal is already saturated with the blood of too many brave men and drenched with the tears of too many survivors." The circular called for a halt in production for a six-day period of mourning for the dead miners.

Four days later, a wrathful Lewis appeared before the House Labor and Education Committee. "I have not said that J. A. Krug, by an affirmative act, killed these men. I say that J. A. Krug, by his inaction, has permitted them to die while he withheld from them succor that it was within his power to grant." The Bureau of Mines had promulgated a safety code, Lewis said. "And we have asked Mr. Krug to enforce his own regulations, which he has failed to do. . . .

"If we must grind up human flesh and bones in an industrial machine that we call modern America, then, before God, I assert that those who consume coal, and you and I, who benefit from that service, because we live in comfort, owe protection to these men first, and we owe security to their families after, if they die."

He concluded, "I say it. I voice it. I proclaim it, and I care not who in heaven or hell opposes it."

The Bureau quickly closed 518 mines until they could

be re-inspected. It asked Lewis for the names of other mines that the union considered unsafe. No coal mine is safe, Lewis replied, if it is violating the Federal safety code. He produced the Bureau's own figures showing that among 3,345 mines inspected in 1946, only 2 were clear of violations. Lewis suggested closing all but those 2. Once the memorial period ended, local mine-safety committees cooperated in the inspection work, and the miners returned to work as the mines were found to be safe.

Once more, the Coal Mines Administration brought the union and employers together in an effort to bring about an agreement and end Government operation. The negotiations went on in the growing shadow of Congressional consideration of the new Taft–Hartley Act. The new bituminous and anthracite contracts that finally emerged in midsummer attempted to squirm around some of the new restrictions in the drastically revised labor-relations law. They were achieved, Lewis said, despite the "slave Taft–Hartley law" which was intended only to reduce "the workers of America to second-class citizens."

21 /

Lewis, the Taft-Hartley Act, and Pensions

"The agreement is now honored"

In Miami, on January 24, 1946, the United Mine Workers rejoined the AFL. Lewis handed AFL President Green a paid-up UMW card, marking Green's more than fifty years of "continuous" membership. Even during the nine years that the miners had been out of the Federation, Lewis said, Green's friends had maintained his membership.

"These boys have been my friends," Green responded, "and I didn't know it. They have been paying my union dues for me all this time."

The reunion had been delayed. Lewis had first applied in the midst of the 1943 soft-coal strike. The application had been entombed in a Federation committee. A year later, Lewis angrily demanded return of the UMW's 60,000 dollar check for advance dues. He accused the AFL of "an amazing exhibition of base hypocrisy approximating moral turpitude." Admission had been denied, he charged, under the "imperative instructions" of New Deal politicians. In 1946, however, in the interest of labor unity, the union leaders said, it was accomplished without fuss and with a small fanfare.

Soon afterwards, the 80th Congress, the first Republican Congress since Herbert Hoover had taken the oath of office eighteen years before, tackled the job of rewriting the nation's labor-relations laws. The House Committee on Education and Labor, after lengthy and often one-sided hearings, concluded: ". . . as a result of labor laws ill-conceived and disastrously executed, the American workingman has been deprived of his dignity as an individual. He has been cajoled, coerced, intimidated, and on many occasions beaten up, in the name of the splendid aims" of the Wagner Act. A minority of the committee warned that the proposed bill not only wiped out labor's gains under the Roosevelt Administration but "turns the clock of history back at least a century and a half." Despite a desperate last-minute campaign by the nation's unions and President Truman's veto, the Taft–Hartley Act became law.

The act extended the idea of unfair labor practices to unions themselves. The Wagner Act had confined them to the actions of an employer. The Taft–Hartley Act prohibited strikes to enforce a union's claim to certain jobs, usually called jurisdictional strikes. It barred "secondary" boycotts, or strikes directed at other employers who might be aiding a struck employer. It denied organizational and bargaining rights to supervisory employees. It authorized damage suits against unions for violation of contract. It banned contributions to candidates for Federal political office by unions and corporations (though not by wealthy industrialists). Union officers (but not employers) were required to swear under oath that they were not members of the Communist Party or any organization affiliated with it. Failure to sign non-Communist affidavits deprived the union of the help of the National Labor Relations Board. It outlawed the closed shop (where a worker had to be a member of the union before he could be hired). It allowed the union shop (where the worker was required to join the union after being hired), but only when it was endorsed in a Government-conducted, secret-ballot election. (Workers voted for the union shop in such overwhelming numbers in the next few years that this requirement was finally removed from the law.) In all, it was a sweeping revision of the nation's labor law. In countless ways, both large and small, it strengthened the hands of employers in opposing their employees' attempts to organize and bargain collectively.

The AFL demanded immediate repeal. But, in the meantime, should its officers comply with the hated law? Specifically, should they sign non-Communist affidavits? They would have to, if the Federation's directly chartered federal locals were to have the services of the NLRB. The Executive Council proposed a series of amendments stripping the Federation vice presidents of their titles. Only President Green and Secretary-Treasurer George Meany would have to swear they were not Communists. Each of the Executive-Council members would be free to do whatever best suited him and his union. Lewis alone dissented.

Lewis carried his dissent to the Federation convention in the fall of 1947. In an angry and arrogant speech, he called on the unions to boycott the law and defeat the proposed amendments. " 'Thou shalt not muzzle the ox that treadeth out the corn.' So runs the Scriptures," he began in classic Lewis style. But Congress designated fifteen million union members in this country as "cattle that treadeth out the economic corn of our country, and the Congress placed an economic muzzle on each of you. What are you going to do about it? Oh, I see. You are going to change our constitution. God help us!"

The act, he rumbled on in the familiar basso, "is the first, ugly, savage thrust of fascism in America." It makes workers "an inferior class of citizens." It was passed "to oppress labor" and to erect barriers to collective bargaining and to organizing. Though the Executive Council denounces the law and agrees it will do nothing to make it "virtuous," yet the leaders of the Federation are among the first "to put their tails between their legs and run like cravens."

If these amendments were adopted, he went on, he would not be a candidate for re-election. That was no threat, he said; he was not holding a gun to the convention's head. "I don't think the Federation has a head," he added. "I think its neck has just grown up and haired over."

Secretary Meany replied that the problem could not be solved by "impugning the integrity of men who feel that they can best represent their membership by complying with the law of the land." Whether the delegates liked it or not, he said, it was on the statute books. The proposed amendments would allow federal locals to make their own decisions, just as Executive-Council members would be free to make their decisions. In any case, the federal locals had neither the experience nor the money to make the fight against the law.

Then Meany met Lewis head-on. As president of the United Mine Workers, Meany said, Lewis upheld with his right hand his union's firm stand against communism. With his left, he made "fellowship" with "the striking America haters who love Moscow." Meany promised, "I am prepared to sign a non-Communist affidavit. I am prepared to go further and sign an affidavit that I never was a comrade to the comrades." Meany carried the day; the amendments were adopted. Soon after, Lewis scribbled a note:

> Green, AFL
> We disaffiliate.
> Lewis

Soon afterward, the miners found themselves entangled once more in a bitter, snarling dispute with the operators. Lewis had proposed a pension of 100 dollars a month for every miner over sixty with at least twenty years in the mines. The neutral trustee of the welfare and retirement fund had resigned; the employer trustee, Ezra Van Horn, refused to accept Lewis's proposal. Lewis wrote the miners on March 12, 1948, that for eight months the coal operators "have dishonored" their agreement. "The United Mine Workers of America might have the idea, the old-fashioned idea," he told reporters, "that agreements are made to be kept—not destroyed, not breached." Lewis's official circular suggested that the miners might want to discuss the matter in their local unions. Almost at once, the men began leaving the pits.

Cyrus Ching, director of the Federal Mediation Service and a former official of United States Rubber Company, called Lewis into a meeting with the operators.

"Obviously, you think time is expendable," Lewis said. "The group of individuals you have asked to your Monday meeting" is "a false front for the coal industry." But, he added, "out of courtesy," the Mine Workers would attend.

Ching recommended—and President Truman promptly appointed—a fact-finding board. Lewis objected. The only question, he insisted, was whether the existing agreement should be honored. The board, nevertheless, invited Lewis to testify. Lewis replied that he was "disinclined" to attend. "It is a logical assumption that the cavilings of the Bar and Bench in their attempt to explicate this infamous enactment [the Taft–Hartley Act] will consume a tedious time."

Beyond that, Lewis charged, two members of the board were prejudiced—one, he charged, could not determine "the distinction between a fact and a scruple." As for Ching, the third member, he was "a truly remarkable man," Lewis said, "who sees through the eyes of United States Rubber."

The board promptly subpoenaed Lewis. He ignored its order. The next morning he was hailed into court and formally ordered to show up. He did, Lewis reported to the miners, "and made answer to all questions asked of me."

He explained that the dispute resulted from "a variance of opinion" between himself and Ezra Van Horn—"no plan Van"—the employer trustee. He had reported the situation to the miners on March 12 but had issued

Coal miners' union meeting in a schoolroom, c. 1947. *National Archives (USIA)*

no further communications. Is it true, he was asked, that by March 16 all the mines were closed?

"I get my information from the newspapers like everyone else does," he replied. "I think the miners may have come to the conclusion that they had been sold a goldbrick."

The next day, Lewis reminded the union's members, "You are not now under any orders, directions, or suggestions, expressed or implied, from me or any of the union officers to cease work or to continue to cease work in protest to the present dishonoring (as we see it) of the 1947 contract."

On April 3, President Truman ordered Attorney General Clark to obtain a court order sending the miners back to work. Judge Goldsborough promptly issued a temporary order without pausing for a hearing. Then, U. S. Senator Styles Bridges of New Hampshire was named neutral trustee. On April 12, by a vote of two-to-one, the fund began paying pensions. Lewis wired all local unions: "Pensions granted. The agreement is now honored." Then the miners went back to work.

But, to Judge Goldsborough, the end of the walkout was not enough. On April 20, for a second time, he found Lewis and the union guilty of contempt of court. He fined the union 1,400,000 dollars, Lewis 20,000 dollars. The Supreme Court later sustained his decisions and the fines.

Contract negotiations in 1948 opened right on the heels of the pension dispute. "We sit here under attainder," Lewis told the operators. "In reverse, your limbs are unshackled. You have no fear of the thought police, and when annoyed by our conduct, you can, at will, invoke additional processes of government to dragoon us. Free collective bargaining? You have reduced the words to mockery."

The miners expected improvements, he told them. "You and your industry are magnificently opulent. . . . From time to time you raise outcries against the men who mine your coal; and, while the gullible public is bewildered by your outcries, you pluck more doubloons from the consumers of coal. In this fashion, and with hardened conscience, you have become the most corpulent of our native fat cats."

In mid-June, the operators walked out of the talks. Trustee Van Horn filed a fourth suit in an effort to tie up the welfare and retirement fund. President Truman appointed another board. On the day Lewis was to appear before the board, Judge Goldsborough handed down a decision upholding the Lewis–Bridges pension plan and rejecting Van Horn's latest complaint. "There seems nothing that shocks the mind," the judge ruled, "at the idea that the members of the United Mine Workers who have worked for twenty years under the ground and are sixty-two years old should get a 100 dollars a month pension. . . . It is just enough to give them a little dignity. The court does not think that there is any justification in law or sound reason for this complaint."

Three days later, the miners and operators signed a new contract. It raised the miner's pay 1 dollar a day. It added 10 cents a ton to the welfare and retirement royalty—now a total of 20 cents. Van Horn was instructed to drop his fourth attempt to tie up the fund.

In the presidential campaign that year, Lewis ignored Dewey, whom he had supported four years before. Truman, he said, was "totally unfitted." After Truman's upset victory, someone suggested appointing Lewis ambassador to Moscow. "I wouldn't appoint John L. Lewis dogcatcher," the testy little President responded.

That would call for a new department, Lewis replied. "The President could ill afford to have more brains in the Dog Department than in the Department of State."

22

The United Mine Workers in Court

"A sort of Marengo. . . ."

"If evil days come on the industry again," Lewis warned the miners' convention in 1948, "you'll find the United Mine Workers moving in. And if there is only three days' work for this industry, then we'll have only three days' work. And if we are going to starve in this industry at any time, we'll just all starve together."

In the summer of 1949, Lewis called for a one-week work stoppage. He labeled it "a brief stabilizing period of inaction." The miners' "magnificent production efforts," he declared, threatened to rock the industry. Hundreds of thousands of men worked short and irregular weeks. Still, there was more than enough production to satisfy both domestic and foreign markets. A week after the members returned to work, the union instituted a three-day work week in all the mines east of the Mississippi River—in effect, an on-again, off-again strike. It was Lewis's effort to share the work equally among the men, at the same time slowing production to match the lagging demand for coal.

The three-day week stretched into early fall. In retaliation, the southern operators stopped royalty payments to the welfare fund. The trustees were finally forced to suspend pension payments and disability and death benefits. The miners protested in their customary way: they quit work.

Leaders of the operators, Lewis said, were so successful in opposing the three-day work week that they had now established a "no-day work week." Powerful financial interests were dictating the coal companies' policy, Lewis claimed; the industrial giants were determined not to yield to the striking steelworkers' demands for a welfare fund like that of the miners. The union called a short truce in the strike, then went back to a three-day week. The major employers replied with a demand that the Government seek a Taft-Hartley injunction that would end the union-imposed three-day week.

Lewis objected. The only issue, he said, was whether the miner would be paid $14.05 a day as the operators wanted or $15 as the union asked. "Should the machinery of the State and the money of its citizens be utilized to oppress the mine workers and cripple their union, merely to save the prosperous coal operators ninety-five cents per day?"

President Truman suggested that while the National Labor Relations Board reviewed certain of the union demands, both sides lay their cases before a fact-finding board. Meanwhile, the miners would return to work. Lewis declined. The miners, he said, "do not wish three strangers, however well-intentioned but necessarily ill-informed, to fix their wages and working conditions." Truman named a board anyway.

The board asked George Love, president of Pittsburgh Consolidation Coal Company, how the bargaining had gone. Love quoted Lewis as saying, "You have the mines. I hold the men in the palm of my hand. What am I bid?"

Lewis exploded. "That is a dirty, deliberate, infamous lie. . . . I say it to you, George Love. You are a liar by the clock."

Love complained that Lewis had never presented the operators with any demands. Lewis replied that the miners knew the operators had no intention of reaching an agreement. The operators believed, Lewis charged, that "they only had to refuse until they got themselves a yellow-dog injunction under this damnable Taft–Hartley Act." Lewis was asked if the union would negotiate any issue. "But yes, but yes, but yes, sir," Lewis replied. "I don't suggest that the Mine Workers will immediately become halfwitted the minute the operators throw some absurd thing on the table, but we will analyze it with them."

In the face of the nearly nationwide stoppage, the Justice Department, at Truman's direction, obtained an injunction ordering the men back to work and the union back to the bargaining table. Lewis wired all district presidents to carry out the Court's instructions and "cease this strike." The miners ignored the instructions. Lewis sent a second wire. "Cease forthwith all stoppages and return to work without delay." The miners refused.

In March, for the third time, Lewis and the Mine Workers faced charges of contempt of court. The Government complained that the union had demonstrated only "token compliance" with the Court's order. "It is simply unreasonable to assume that 372,000 men in 28 different states could have acted as individuals in exactly the same way and at exactly the same time." It was not at all unreasonable, the union's attorney, Welly Hopkins, replied. The miners were angry; they simply laid down their tools and refused to work. The union was equally disappointed in their refusal to end the strike.

Judge R. B. Keech cleared the union. He conceded that the walkout may have been encouraged in some way that was not in the record, but he could not convict the union on mere conjecture. Then President Truman asked Congress for power to seize the mines, for the sixth time in seven years.

A few days later, George Love was summoned from a meeting of operators. He returned shortly to announce that he and Lewis had concluded an agreement that his company could accept. It gave the miners a pay raise of 70 cents a day. The welfare and retirement royalty was increased another 10 cents a ton—to a total of 40 cents—and the operators agreed to make up the defaulted welfare-fund payments. The contract would recognize the miners' right to refuse to work when they were convinced the operators were not acting in good faith.

It had been a long, costly, and painful struggle, "a sort of Marengo," Lewis said, referring to one of Napoleon's costly victories. "The mine workers emerged . . . with additional bread and butter money for their families, with additional life and death money for their sick and ailing . . . with their union intact, with their membership unimpaired, and with all labor benefited by the discrediting of the Taft–Hartley abomination." It also marked, as it turned out, the beginning of a period of cooperation and peace in the coal industry.

23

Fringe Benefits for the Miners

"Through our own strength we triumphed"

"Miners are haunted men. Their minds are vexed with the memories of bloody struggles for higher pay and for the preservation and growth of their labor union. Their thoughts are constantly troubled by the insecurity of work, for they know that, although the calendar year contains 365 days, they have worked as little as 142, and only nine times out of the last 25 years have they averaged more than 200 days a year. Their hearts grow weary repressing the importunate warnings of the dangers that lurk underground which may at any time cut them off from their livelihood. Their families silently share these burdens."

These words burst from a page in a *Medical Survey of the Bituminous Coal Industry,* conducted in 1946 under the terms of the Krug–Lewis agreement. They supplied a backdrop to the survey's grim findings on the miners' squalid living conditions, on the incompetent and dishonest medical care they often received, on the monotony, inadequacy, and the sheer filth of many company towns.

The miners had long complained that they were being cheated in the medical care they received from company doctors and company-controlled hospitals. A union spokesman told a national health conference in 1938 that over 8 million dollars was being checked off miners' pay for doctor and hospital services. He estimated that miners could be given a model, comprehensive health service for 6 million dollars, with millions left over for research, mental hygiene, and child guidance.

Miners paid for medical care out of their pockets as well as by checkoffs from their pay. The checkoff paid for hospitalization, though standards were low and hospitals frequently inaccessible. Lewis often cited a hospital in Utah that was 160 miles from the mine. Miners made monthly payments for medical service, accident insurance, and the burial fund. They bought their own dental care, paid extra for drugs and vaccines, and to have their children delivered. Operators were indifferent. Only after a strike and Government seizure of the mines had a welfare fund been established and a long overdue survey undertaken of health conditions, housing, and sanitation in the coal fields.

Rear Admiral Joel T. Boone led the team that surveyed 260 mines in 22 coal-producing states. The report, published in 1947, charged the operators with failure to maintain decent sanitary housing in company-owned camps. They tolerated disease-breeding creeks (raw sewage often turned them into open sewers) and poor disposal of garbage. First-aid supplies, facilities, and services were inadequate. Mine sanitation was neglected. Less than half of the mines provided washhouses; half of those charged the men an average of $1.15 a month for their upkeep. Water supplies at 120 mines were pol-

A company-owned town. *Bureau of Mines, U.S. Department of the Interior*

luted by industrial waste, mine water, or untreated sewage. About nine of every ten company houses were of frame construction, usually of the "cheapest materials." Only one house in ten had a complete bathroom with a shower or tub. Only one in twenty had sewage collection systems; 6 percent had septic tanks.

Company and hospital domination of medical and hospitalization plans, the survey found, too often resulted in abuse, neglect, and indifference. Operators used the miners' medical checkoff to pay the company doctor for services for which the company itself should have paid. Patients were often treated in dirty, ill-equipped offices. Many doctors were untrained or poorly trained. Hospitals were often small, badly equipped, understaffed, and overcrowded. Three-quarters of them were inadequate.

"If it is the custom and tradition that mine families shall exist in squalor," the survey report declared, "it is time for that custom and tradition to be abolished."

At their convention in 1960, Lewis reminded the miners that a welfare fund had been created in the mining industry in 1946 for the first time in the seven hundred years that the English-speaking world had been digging coal. By 1960, the fund had paid out 1,464,000,000 dollars in benefits. "I am not sure that I know just what a billion is," he added, "but whatever it is, we have had it, and our people received it in benefits."

The fund's medical work began with a program of rehabilitation for paraplegic miners—men whose backs had been broken or whose spinal cords had been severed in mine accidents. Services were also offered for victims of chronic chest diseases, such as silicosis. In 1949, the fund arranged with hospitals, physicians, dentists, and pharmacists for a program of general medical care for the miners and their families. The fund built ten hospitals, later turned over to a church-sponsored operating

Conditions in a company house. *Bureau of Mines, U.S. Department of the Interior*

group. It helped to develop a number of group health plans that served some sections of the general community as well as the miners.

Safety on the job held a place alongside wages and

welfare in the union's goals. Lewis opened the anthracite negotiations in 1925 with this greeting, "Since I last met you in conference, one thousand of my people have been killed in your collieries and more than forty thousand have been maimed and injured." Twenty years later, he soberly asked the bituminous operators, "Were you ever in a company house where a family lives when the breadwinner is carried in dead?"

He chilled the blood of many congressional committees with vivid descriptions of the miners' dead. To one committee, he reported 300,000 "mine-made victims" in a five-year period. "Some died—more than six thousand. Some lived; some lived blind, some with twisted backs, lost limbs, paralyzed bodies, broken bones, the flesh burned from their faces until they are grinning spectres of men." He once proposed a parade of "maimed, mangled and butchered" miners, the walking injured dragging the dead, "so that Congress might see."

Lewis frequently lambasted the operators with the industry's job-accident statistics. Every single miner, he argued in 1946, has been injured statistically twice—and he gambled whether his injuries laid him up for a shift or incapacitated him for life. (There were times when Lewis used the figures less to make the mines safe than to win higher pay; they put the operators on the defensive.)

Mining at best was hazardous. Walls gave way, the roof caved in. Men were crushed and killed in the underground traffic, caught unaware on the tracks between train and entry or while coupling cars. Gas and dust exploded with untold violence; fire exhausted the oxygen and charred their bodies. Still, union officials insistently maintained that while coal mining was "notoriously hazardous and unhealthy," it need not be.

Once the union regained its place in the industry, it launched a drive for tougher Federal safety laws. In 1941, Congress gave the Bureau of Mines authority to make annual or "necessary" inspections and to publish its findings. Lewis used the murderous explosion at Centralia to expose the weaknesses of the law. Then, just before Christmas, 1951, a disaster at Orient Number 2 at West Frankfort, Illinois, killed 119 miners. "How many shocks," Lewis asked a Congressional committee, "does it take to move us?"

The following summer, Congress passed another safety law, which, for the first time, gave Bureau of Mines inspectors power to shut down unsafe mines. On the heels of it, Lewis proclaimed another National Memorial Period. The union's declaration reminded miners of the "yuletide horror" of the West Frankfort disaster. In the six months since, 334 miners had been killed, 20,000 maimed. The union pointed to over 52,000 violations of the safety code reported by Federal inspectors—29,000 of them repeat violations, 38,000 still uncorrected. It called on management to put each mine in legally safe condition. It instructed union safety committees to make available any number of men for making the mines safe, though coal production was halted for the ten-day period.

After 1947, the UMW stood aside from the two major

Picture taken of Mr. Lewis (December 21, 1951) after he emerged from Orient Number 2 Mine following the explosion that killed 119 men. *Wayne State University Labor History Archives*

labor federations, but Lewis maintained his highly personal interest in labor unity. When the Korean conflict broke out, the two federations formed the United Labor Policy Committee. The UMW was left out. Lewis wrote to Green, apologizing for disturbing "the calm placidity of your ordered existence." But, he went on, since the AFL had excluded the miners from the unity conference, he wanted Green to know that ". . . any mess that you cook up with the CIO, if you can cook up any mess with the CIO, will of course have to be eaten by you, and you alone. We do our own cooking." The miners would not be bound by Green's or the Committee's commitments. "We do our own committing." Nor would the miners be bound by Green's or the Committee's no-strike pledge. "We do our own no-striking."

At one point, Lewis proposed a 50 million dollar labor defense fund. The miners would put up 10 million dollars if forty other unions would put up 1 million dollars each. It would serve as "a simple insurance proposition to be available to any union engaged in economic struggle." There were no takers. When the steelworkers struck in 1952, Lewis put 10 million dollars to their credit in a Washington bank. The *Journal* reported a month later that the credit was neither used nor publicly acknowledged.

Lewis suggested still another unity conference in 1952. George Meany commented that if Lewis wanted action on the subject of labor unity, ". . . he is quite familiar with the process of returning to the AFL. He is also quite familiar with the process of leaving the AFL."

In the spring of 1954, Lewis sounded a jarring note. The miners joined with the teamsters and the steelworkers, two of the nation's most powerful unions, in a well-publicized "triple alliance." Their purpose, they said, was to "combat rising unemployment and to assist one another" with legislative problems. The alliance might have become a potent rival to the two major federations but, though further meetings were reportedly planned, the alliance soon lapsed.

Lewis was dubious when the AFL and CIO finally merged in 1955. The merger, he thought, gave unwarranted power to "a small group of men" and threatened the welfare of smaller unions. "I greatly fear that the new merger will part like the rope of sand that it is." As time went on, Lewis's doubts grew, though the "rope of sand" held together. It had brought no new blood into organizing the unorganized, he said in 1958. Nor did he think it had any business trying to regulate the morals of the labor movement. Expulsion of great unions—the AFL–CIO had just expelled the Teamsters—"because of the peccadilloes, immoral or otherwise, of certain individual officers is merely shooting the dog to remove the tick."

Lewis never spared fellow labor leaders his criticism. He referred to Walter Reuther, head of the auto workers and one of the architects of the AFL–CIO merger, as "chronically inebriated, I should think, by the exuberance of his own verbosity." (Lewis had used almost the same words during an NRA hearing 20 years before to describe an employer.) He dismissed Meany as ". . . an honest plumber trying to abolish sin in the labor movement." (Meany had commented earlier that Lewis would have wrecked the unity discussions. "You can't live with that man—you can only live under him.")

But Lewis held back in the case of James R. Hoffa, the frequently beleaguered president of the teamsters. Lewis explained, "I don't join the mob every time it hollers 'Stop, thief.' . . . He is entitled to have his chance, under our flag, under our law, and to have an equal break before his peers." He told a House committee that for years he had been "the whipping boy." Now it was Hoffa.

Lewis never forgave Senator Robert A. Taft for his part in the Taft–Hartley law. When Taft was running for re-election in 1950, Lewis asked the head of the Ohio mine operators to bar him from the mines. Taft's "disagreeable" presence, he said, could enrage the men to a point of evacuation of the mines. To a Senate committee he described the working of the law, "Oh, most injurious, most destructive, most costly, most harassing, most disturbing."

Later, under the impact of a Senate committee investigating allegations of graft and corruption in unions, Congress was considering tightening the labor laws still further. Lewis objected. The proposals discriminated against unions, he asserted, while ignoring other voluntary associations. Unions were no more crooked than bankers. He once looked up the statistics in several coal-producing states, he claimed, and found that proportionally more bankers were in jail than miners. The bill, he warned, in fact aimed at wiping out unions. Why not, he proposed, simply write a bill making it unlawful for an American to join a labor union. "Damn the chains," he cried, "and those who advocate them."

The years moved on. New contracts, peacefully negotiated, raised the miners' pay from $14.75 to $16.35 a day in 1951, and to $18.25 in 1952, $20.25 in 1955, $22.25 in 1956, and $24.25 in 1958. The welfare-fund royalty was maintained at 40 cents a ton. Vacations were stretched to fourteen days, the vacation payment to 200 dollars. Company towns, in time, vanished from the scene and, with them, many of the shameful conditions they had produced.

Looking back, in 1959, Lewis noted that the industry had made progress in modernizing. "The operators came to the realization that common-sense procedures were better than the old methods." Not that there weren't close calls.

In 1952, during the Korean conflict, Lewis negotiated a raise of $1.90 a day. The Wage Stabilization Board cut back the increase to $1.40 a day. With the possibility of a strike mounting rapidly, President Truman summoned the union and employers to the White House. Afterward, Lewis dispatched a letter to the operators. "We have a contract. It is with your Association. It is complete. It speaks for itself. You signed it. It was negotiated in the American way—through collective bargaining. It is as pure as a sheep's heart."

Lewis gave blunt notice that the miners expected the operators to respect the agreement. For his part, President Truman directed the Wage Stabilization Board to restore the full increase. Failure to do so, he said, would provoke a strike. There was no emergency at the moment but he did not want to create a problem that would reach its peak about the time General Eisenhower took over the White House. It was a "unique situation."

More often, the agreements seemed to conform to Lewis's description of the 1955 agreement. It "will not oppress the coal consumers, nor yet expose the brittle bones of the operators to the icy blasts of the coming winter . . . a constructive instrument with edible virtues. Mine workers require strong meat and eating money will produce more coal than philosophic discussion." When local walkouts threatened the peace, Lewis took steps. "Carry this message back to your members," he told the delegates to the 1956 convention. "Don't do it again."

Once upon a time, an operator had told a group of miners, "We won't give you any better terms than we are offering because we can't; and we can't because we won't. What the hell are you going to do about it?" Discussing the 1956 contract settlement, Lewis commented that times had changed. "It was only changed by the unceasing efforts of this union . . . in times of stress and trial, sometimes covering a period of years . . . when everyone was against us except our own people. Through our own strength we triumphed."

A dramatically changed industry testified to the triumph. More than 600,000 men had manned the nation's coal mines in World War I. The number fell to 442,000 in World War II, about twenty-five years later. In 1960, the work force was under 190,000. The average miner produced 3.78 tons of coal a day in 1918, 6.3 tons in 1949, 13 tons in 1960.

The drastic slash in the work force resulted partly from a falling demand for coal. The nation used close to 700 million tons at the peak of its demand; in 1960 it needed only 416 million tons. It resulted, too, from machines taking over more and more of the miner's work. Two thirds of the nation's soft coal was machine cut in 1960, 86 percent of it mechanically loaded, two thirds of it mechanically cleaned. In 1940, less than 10 percent of the output was strip mined; in 1960, nearly a third. Mechanical loaders and conveyors (often fed by branch conveyors) replaced the miner's shovel and dinky mine cars. Continuous mining machines cut and loaded the coal without blasting. Strip mining simply tore away the overburden with increasingly hungry bites. One giant stripping machine uncovered 14,000 tons a day—more than a thousand men could dig. One man controlled it. A new push-button miner was operated from the surface by reading blips on a radar screen. It, too, replaced scores of miners.

American miners' pay in the early sixties was three times the highest rates in Europe, but American miners produced seven times as much coal in a day. American coal could thus be sold at a small fraction of the prices charged in other coal-producing countries. Coal prices at the mine were lower in 1963 than in 1948, despite increased costs all along the line. The increased productivity resulting from mechanization made possible both low prices for the consumer and wage raises for the miner.

In 1951, quizzed by a group of German coal techni-
cians, Lewis said the union had decided years before that
"it is better to have half a million men working in the
industry on good wages . . . than it is to have a million
men working in the industry in poverty and degradation." He did not think, he once told a group of Ford
workers, "that God ever put an idea in the mind of an
inventor for the sole advantage of the employers." The
inventor and stockholder, the workers, the consumer are
entitled to share in the result of increased productivity.
How did you decide each share? "That's where collective
bargaining comes in."

Still, mechanization wiped out jobs with stunning
speed. In the fifties and since, thousands of displaced
miners have been jobless—and worse, hopeless. Parts of
Appalachia were a wasteland peopled by miners without
work and without a future. The human cost of the shift
to machines, thought Reporter A. H. Raskin, was so stag-
gering "that few other unions, surveying the desperate
men in the rotting communities of West Virginia, Pennsylvania, Tennessee and Kentucky, are likely to be in-
spired to go out and do likewise." In recent years, special
government programs sought to rescue the people of
Appalachia from joblessness and the lack of opportunity.
The union sought child-labor laws to keep boys under
seventeen out of the mines. More experienced men were
given preference in jobs; younger men were encouraged
to turn to other industries. Older miners were helped to
retire on the strength of their industry pension and Social
Security benefits.

The union has looked to an expanding economy with full employment to provide jobs for workers displaced by machines and to offer opportunities to the young. Special programs, too, were needed to train or retrain men for different jobs, to encourage workers to move from areas of job scarcity to those where jobs were more numerous. At times, those policies have not been enough to avert unemployment and hardship and sheer want among the displaced miners—one result of the union's policies and the working of the national economy.

Another is one Lewis frequently cited. In Ohio, about the turn of the century, miners worked ten hours underground, traveled an hour and a half to and from the work place in the mine. He received no pay for lunch time. His wage was about a dollar a day. Since then, wages have gone up, hours have been shortened, the welfare and retirement fund established—an increase of about 2,500 percent. The price of coal in that period—up to 1959—has gone up less than 100 percent. "The American coal operators would never have mechanized their mines unless they had been compelled to do so" by the UMW, Lewis declared. "The United Mine Workers of America holds that labor is entitled to a participation in that increased productivity." The UMW not only cooperated in mechanization, he said; "we invented the policy."

The union did not keep men on the jobs to collect dues or retain jobs, Lewis repeatedly said. "It would be a millennium if men do not have to work underground but can all work in God's sunshine. That will be a long time coming but we would be in favor of it."

24

Rewards for a Life of Service to Labor

"... a man of that character"

One day late in December, 1959, the editor of the Mine Workers *Journal* received a phone call. The deep, rumbling voice, unmistakably Lewis's, asked when his next edition closed. Monday, the editor told him. "Well, I may have something for you. I'll let you know." Shortly before the deadline, Lewis sent over a letter addressed to the "Members of the United Mine Workers of America." It announced that he would resign "from the constitutional office of President shortly after the New Year."

His letter spoke words of praise for Vice President Thomas Kennedy who would succeed him. Then he summed up the long years of his office: "At first, your wages were low, your hours long, your labor perilous, your health disregarded, your children without opportunity, your Union weak, your fellow citizens and public representatives indifferent to your wrongs; today... your wages are the highest in the land, your working hours the lowest, your safety more assured, your health guarded, your old age protected, your children equal in opportunity with their generation, and your Union strong."

He returned time and again to the same theme as he

made his way through the inevitable retirement dinners and last appearance, as he transferred his obligations to his successor. Sometimes he joked about his place in the record. "As a matter of fact," he told a retirement dinner, "there hasn't been very much for me to do down through the years except to be very careful to be around when an agreement was signed and get my picture in the paper. . . . And by getting this public mention it made it easier for me to be elected to office from time to time." Sometimes he probed the wellsprings of the union's strength. ". . . Through many dreary and tedious years . . . we have come to an understanding of the fraternity, the loyal affection for each other that is a symbol of the mining industry. This fraternity, more than any other factor in periods of strain, has been responsible for the machinelike, military precision on the part of our membership in sustaining union policy and continuing to face our opposition."

He was practical, even then. He warned against using the generous help of Americans to build foreign industries and foreign economies that would undersell American goods in world markets. He complained again, as he had so often before, about the lot of the unemployed worker. (When newsmen presented him with a scroll at a retirement dinner, Lewis acknowledged it as "a testimonial for what I've done to reduce their unemployment.") He loosed a final angry blast at Congress for shirking its responsibility to strengthen mine safety laws.

The union made him president emeritus and asked him to continue as chairman and trustee of the Welfare and

John L. Lewis visits Ford Local 600, c. 1961. *Wayne State University Labor History Archives*

Retirement Fund and to represent the union on other boards and commissions.

The accolades poured in. There was no longer the old roar of hate, but countless songs of praise instead. "There are stories he was born," Edward J. Lally wrote in the *American Metal Market*. "Chances are he was mined. But the coal preparation plant was never made that could cut him down to size." "A giant," they said, "trailblazer," "an honorable man," "inexorable crusader," "the tallest tree of his time and place," "genuine in his compassion and savage in his attack," "an obdurate, messianic man."

The annual report of Consolidation Coal Company, the nation's largest commercial producer of bituminous coal and an ancient antagonist, called him "a great labor statesman." The head of the soft-coal operators also praised his "statesmanship." Joseph R. Moody, president of the National Coal Policy Conference—an industry

John L. Lewis at Ford Local 600, c. 1961. *Wayne State University Labor History Archives*

body Lewis helped to organize—lauded his "tremendous courage, determination and foresight." George H. Love—Lewis had once labeled him "a liar by the clock"—called him "an extraordinarily fine person."

"Majesty," said *The New York Times,* is the word for Lewis. "In his forty years of labor leadership he has commanded more idolatry and more hatred than any other union chief in the country's history. But even those who damned him most were quick to concede that he was a man of towering personal gifts and that he used them extravagantly. He made his loyal army of coal-diggers the highest-paid and most adequately insured group of industrial workers in the world; he stormed the bastions of the open shop in the mass production industries and led millions of workers in steel, automobiles and other fields into union ranks; he built a pioneer welfare and pension fund that became a model of industry-financed social security.

"And in the process he conducted epic battles with Presidents, members of Congress, industrialists and virtually every other union leader who came to power in his lifetime. He was not a man who believed in speaking softly and he was congenitally unable to accept second place to anyone—even if the 'anyone' held a four-year lease in the White House."

Lewis had passed up chances for political appointments. One biographer said he had been offered a chance to go to the United States Senate. He had been asked to run for Congress. President Coolidge reportedly wanted to make him Secretary of Labor. He had passed up, too, chances to be rich. Instead, he had cast his lot with the

The following letter was received with this picture from Mr. Harden, a retired coal miner.

R.D. #2, Cadiz, Ohio
August 28th, 1963

Dear Mr. Lewis,

I am an old retired grandpa and I'm having a wonderful time. All my life I have wanted to do things but had no time to do them. Now that my days in the mines are over I have lots of time and I'm enjoying myself very much.

One of my pastimes is drawing. I have been doing this since I was a boy in Scotland. I liked your picture in the last U.M.W. Journal and decided to draw you one.

Sincerely,
John Harden

union. He had held off presidents. He once recalled bitterly how frequently the men in the White House had asked him to do what they wanted him to do. "And nine times out of ten," he told the miners, "they wanted me to do something that would disarm you or prevent you from accomplishing something of which you dreamed."

In 1963, on retiring as chairman of the National Coal Policy Commission, Lewis was presented with a portrait of himself. "I would hate," he commented, "on a dark night and in a close place to meet a man of that character." President John F. Kennedy praised his "dignity and integrity" and hoped he would write his memoirs. Lewis replied that he was "overwhelmed by these accusations of good character." (Characteristically, his parting shot expressed astonishment at the "patience" of the nation's 6 million unemployed.)

In 1964, President Lyndon B. Johnson presented him with the nation's highest civilian award, the Medal of Freedom. He was one of a company of thirty, including movie-maker Walt Disney, composer Aaron Copland, pundit Walter Lippmann, author John Steinbeck. "Eloquent spokesman of labor," the citation read, "he has given voice to the aspirations of industrial workers of the country and led the cause of free trade unions with a healthy system of free enterprise."

"Old John L. Lewis may be rough," a miner once said, "but he's always working for us."

Each facet of this complicated man revealed a different Lewis. "I don't give a hang what happened yesterday," he once said. "I live for today and tomorrow. I will say only this: It takes every man some time to find himself in this world, to decide what he wants to do with his life. It took me longer than most people." If there were moments of self-doubt, there were also many, longer moments of certainty. None was more certain than when he stood before a convention of miners and in that unmistakable rumble declared: "As an individual, my opinions and my voice are of no more consequence in the world of affairs, or in the coal industry of the country, than the voice or the opinions of any passerby on the street. It is only when I am able to translate your dreams and aspirations into words that others may understand, that my tongue possesses any strength or my hand has any force." And then, he added, he had never faltered or failed to plead the case of the mine workers, "not in the quavering tones of a feeble mendicant asking alms, but in the thundering voice of the captain of a mighty host, demanding the rights to which free men are entitled."

About the Author

David F. Selvin is editor of *San Francisco Labor,* and has been a consultant in public relations to labor unions. He received his B.S. and M.A. in economics from the University of California at Berkeley, where he lives today with his wife and three sons, the youngest of whom is interested in politics. "Through him," Mr. Selvin writes, "I discovered how little the young people's shelves in our libraries offered anyone interested in the labor movement or its leaders." This led him to write biographies of Sam Gompers, Eugene Debs, and now, John L. Lewis.

Some notes on reading

John L. Lewis's career has been well documented in biographies and histories as well as, day-by-day, in the public prints. He was, most of his active life, a prime newsmaker. The coal industry, too, has been studied, analyzed, diagnosed, and prognosticated until the reports threaten to overflow the library shelves. The literature, in short, offers just as much depth as the reader has strength and will to explore.

John L. Lewis's own views are perhaps better documented in Saul Alinsky, *John L. Lewis* (Putnam's Sons, New York, 1949) than anywhere else. As Murray Kempton noted in *Part of Our Time,* it "contains so much otherwise unpublished Lewis conversation and self-reportage as to amount almost to a memoir." James Wechsler takes a sharply contrasting point of view in *Labor Baron* (Wm. Morrow & Co., New York, 1944), as the title might indicate. McAlister Coleman offers a friendly, more balanced view in *Men and Coal* (Farrar & Rinehart, Inc., New York, 1943). C. L. Sulzberger, *Sit Down With John L. Lewis* (Random House, New York, 1938) is a useful earlier, informal portrait. Cecil Carnes, *John L. Lewis: Leader of Labor* (Robt. Speller Publishing Corp., New York, 1936) is an even earlier, though perhaps less insightful biography.

Lewis, of course, is strongly spotlighted in the McDonald and Lynch history, *Coal and Unionism* (Lynald Books, Silver Springs, Md., 1939), which is a union document. He is the central focus of *John L. Lewis and the International Union,* an outright tribute. John Brophy offers a qualified view in *A Miner's Life* (University of Wisconsin Press, Madison, 1964). The left-wing view of Lewis is reflected in works of the early thirties by Anna Rochester, *Labor and Coal* (International Publishers, New York, 1931); Bruce Minton and John Stuart, *Men Who Lead Labor* (Modern Age Books, New York, 1937). Lewis's own book, *The Miner's Fight for American Standards* (Bell Publishing Co., Indianapolis, 1925) sheds some diffused light on Lewis's economic ideas but precious little on Lewis the man.

For the historical setting, the reader should turn to the more casual *Labor on the March* (University Books, New York, 1938 [1950]) by Edward Levinson; the infinitely detailed study of Walter Galenson, *The CIO Challenge to the AFL* (Harvard University Press, Cambridge, 1960); the more general survey of Philip Taft, *Organized Labor in American History* (Harper & Row, New York, 1964). Levinson's is more reportorial in nature, since he was both a reporter and labor editor. The Galenson and Taft histories are more scholarly and more formidable. Irving Bernstein combines readability and scholarship in *The Lean Years* (Houghton Mifflin Co., Boston, 1940), a study of the period from 1920 to 1933.

Lewis is shown in a variety of ways, too, in biographies, autobiographies, histories of various kinds—Sidney Hillman, David Dubinsky, Franklin Delano Roosevelt, William Hutcheson, Frances Perkins, to name only a few—and in studies of the coal industry by Homer L. Morris, Morton S. Baratz, Edward A. Wieck, Carter Goodrich, and many more.

I made extensive use of the *Journal* of the United Mine Workers. Its several editors, in their individual ways, ably reflected the viewpoints of the union's leadership and the union's struggles. It was an invaluable source.

Government documents offer a veritable mine of information. I have used, in parts, studies by various coal commissions, by the Boone medical-survey team, the publications of the Bureau of

Mines, and records of hearings before various Congressional bodies. The seam runs far deeper and wider than I have been able to dig.

To all those involved in this vast literature—to the authors and editors, the researchers, statisticians, economists, reporters, and rewrite men, I am immeasurably indebted. Without their work, mine would have been impossible. I offer them this inadequate and blanket, but earnest, word of thanks. Needless, perhaps, to add, the responsibility for the accuracy of my work, its point of view, and its conclusions are my own.

DAVID F. SELVIN

Berkeley, California
June, 1968

Index